"I AIN'T SORRY FOR NOTh;N' I DONe"

"i AiN't SORRY FOR NOthiN' i DONe"

August Wilson's
Process of Playwriting

•

JOAN HERRINGTON

LIMELIGHT EDITIONS • NEW YORK

Library of Congress Cataloging-in-Publication Data

Herrington, Joan, 1960–
        I ain't sorry for nothin' I done: August Wilson's process of
    playwriting / Joan Herrington.—1st Limelight ed.
        p.   cm.
    Includes bibliographical references and index.
    ISBN 0-87910-270-5
        1. Wilson, August—Criticism and interpretation. 2. Historical
    drama, American—History and criticism. 3. Afro-Americans in
    literature. 4. Wilson, August—Technique. 5. Playwriting.
    I. Title.
    PS3573.I45677Z68 1998
        812'.54–dc21   98-27228   CIP

Acknowledgements

I am grateful to the many people who have supported my work on this book. First and foremost, I thank August Wilson who gave so generously of his time, provided unlimited access to his work, and opened himself to me. I hope that through this book others can share his work, his life, and his vision for the world.

I also acknowledge, with deep appreciation, the insights provided by the many actors, directors, dramaturgs, and other theater artists whom I interviewed for this book.

In addition, my gratitude goes to my colleagues in the Theatre Department at Western Michigan University, my Chair, Dr. D. Terry Williams, and Dean Robert Luscombe, for encouraging my work on this book.

Finally, and most importantly, I thank my family—my two daughters, Emily and Sarah, who patiently shared their mother with these pages, and my husband, Rick, whose selflessness and faith enabled me to complete "*I Ain't Sorry for Nothin' I Done.*"

Contents

Illustrations follow page 72.

The Process of Playwriting

Introduction

In an old pile of 78 rpm records he came across in a dime store one day in 1965, August Wilson spotted Bessie Smith's "Nobody in Town Can Bake a Jelly Roll Like Mine." He bought it, put it on his turntable, and played it twenty-two times.

> It is difficult to describe what happened to me...For the first time some one was speaking directly to me about myself and the cultural environment of my life. I was stunned. By its beauty. By its honesty. And most important by the fact that it was mine. An affirmation of my presence in the world that would hold me up and give me ground to stand on. I began to look at the occupants of my [rooming] house in a different light. I saw behind the seeming despair and emptiness of their lives a force of life, and an indomitable will that linked to their historical precedents became noble in a place where nobility wasn't supposed to exist.[1]

This awakening to Bessie Smith and the blues had a profound effect on Wilson who began writing to explore, in his own words, the nobility of those lives, first in poetry and later in plays. Equally

1

influential in the development of Wilson's creative world view were three other artists: the painter Romare Bearden, the playwright Amiri Baraka, and the Argentinean short-story writer Jorge Luis Borges. Along with the blues, they constitute what Wilson refers to as his "four B's."

The intricate interplay of social, political, and metaphysical thought, which is the defining characteristic of all four of Wilson's "B's," opened up a world of artistic possibility for him, and provided a succession of aural and visual images which serve as his primary inspiration. Wilson's plots, style, structure, and underlying themes all bear the marks of these formative influences, three of which are African American.

Despite Wilson's focus on the African-American experience, however, his work crosses racial and cultural boundaries, reaching a large and diverse audience. As noted by Sandra Shannon, Wilson's appeal is the product of his ability to create drama which simultaneously combines W.E.B. DuBois' call for drama which contained "the Negro as subject and object," and Alan Locke's plan for black theater artists to "interpret the soul of their people in a way to win the attention and admiration of the world." [2] Wilson is the first African-American playwright to be consistently produced in mainstream American theater. In ten years, six of his plays have had successful Broadway productions, and he has twice received the Pulitzer Prize for Drama.

This book analyzes Wilson's success by exploring the unique evolution of his first three major plays, *Ma Rainey's Black Bottom*, *Fences*, and *Joe Turner's Come and Gone*, the writing of which defined Wilson's unique creative process, and also *Jitney*, Wilson's most recent project, through which he has redefined his creative process. Where does the work begin? On what does Wilson draw? How does he create the first draft? What happens step-by-step as he refines his work? Through what method does he hone and shape his words into drama that speaks to so many thousands of people? The answers explain how Wilson incorporates disparate influences, balances conflicting impulses within himself, juggles contradictory input from colleagues and critics, and ultimately speaks with a singular and powerful voice.

Of the four "B's," the painter Romare Bearden has had the

most direct impact on Wilson's work. Wilson remembers clearly his discovery of Romare Bearden:

> My friend Claude Purdy had purchased a copy of *The Prevalence of Ritual*, and one night in the fall of 1977, after dinner and much talk, he laid it open on the table before me. "Look at this," he said. "Look at this." I looked. What for me had been so difficult, Bearden made seem so simple, so easy. It was the art of a large and generous spirit that defined not only the character of black American life, but also its conscience.[3]

Images from three Bearden collage paintings and silk screens— *Continuities, Mill Hand's Lunch Bucket* and *The Piano Lesson*— inspired Wilson to create plays around the characters pictured at their centers. Then, Wilson drew on Bearden's methodology as well as his imagery, assembling his plays from a collage of disparate elements which together formed a cohesive whole more powerful than its individual components. Wilson also drew upon a stockpile of recurring visual images that Bearden had used to symbolize the collective history of black people in America: trains, birds, conjure women, et al.

One of these recurring images is that of the black musician, which in Wilson's drama finds an aural component in the music of the blues. *Ma Rainey's Black Bottom*, which is set in the twenties and concerns the trials of the legendary blues singer, is merely the most obvious reflection of the influence of the blues on Wilson's work. But all his plays, to varying degrees, share a blues sensibility, a blues singer's view of the human condition, with all that there is to commiserate and celebrate. Many of them also incorporate song titles and lyrics in their dialogue.

Another of Wilson's influences, the playwright Amiri Baraka, was also a student of the blues, both as music and as cultural history. Inspired by Baraka's political activism and aggressive style of playwriting, Wilson experimented early in his career with plays that clearly resembled those of his predecessor who had been at the forefront of the African-American theater movement of the 1960s. Ultimately, Wilson's combination of realism and spiritual-

3

ism moved him away from Baraka stylistically, but he continued to explore one of Baraka's central themes—the ongoing conflict between revolution and assimilation.

Baraka called for a theater that would force change, a theater of revolution, and at the core of many of his early plays, those that most influenced Wilson, is a central character who violently stands up for himself in the face of his oppressor. And Baraka's plays often include a physical embodiment of oppressive white society—someone who can be killed, as Baraka often advocated. Wilson's plays also portray the struggle for human dignity. But the confrontation undertaken by Wilson's characters is more spiritual than visceral, with the offender often represented in non-physical form. In *Ma Rainey's Black Bottom*, Levee rails against a God who did not stop the rape of his mother; in *The Piano Lesson*, Boy Willie wrestles with the ghost of the man who enslaved his forefathers; in *Joe Turner's Come and Gone*, Loomis challenges Jesus Christ; and in *Fences*, Troy beckons Mr. Death. Although the rage of Wilson's characters is just as powerful as that of Baraka's, they do not remedy their oppression through violence. Instead, each must wage an internal battle for self-definition and formulate an individual response to oppression before he can face external foes. Some succeed; some do not.

As Wilson moves the struggle of his characters from a physical to a metaphysical plane, he exhibits the influence of the Argentinean essayist and short-story writer Jorge Luis Borges. In the writings of Borges, the central characters strive to understand a seemingly incomprehensible world. Borges' tales are often fantastic and, on the surface, seem to bear no resemblance to Wilson's work. But both men write of man's need to fulfill his destiny and understand his place within a historical continuum.

Borges and Wilson are more concerned with how things happen than with what actually happens. Wilson was specifically influenced by Borges' technique of revealing the ending of his stories in the first lines, which forces the reader to focus on the process and not the outcome. Thus, Wilson's most recent play, *Seven Guitars*, begins at the end of the story.

Borges' subversive styles and transcendental themes support Wilson's preference for a theatrical style that does not follow

4

traditional western dramatic progression toward climax and resolution — a preference exhibited in Wilson's early work and again in his most recent plays. Abandoning linear structure, Wilson weaves and reweaves images and motifs, steeping his audience in complex characters and their relationships.

Indeed, early drafts of all of Wilson's plays are consistent in their inclusion of extensive storytelling, non-realistic dramatic elements, and a sprawling narrative. But by the time Wilson's plays reach Broadway, they have become much more akin to traditional western drama. The step-by-step process of revision Wilson applies to each of his plays results in a melding of his original artistic impulses with mainstream theatrical conventions and it reveals his creative response to the very commercial system within which plays are developed in the American theater. Wilson's conflict and resolution are perhaps an artistic equivalent of the conflict examined by the plays themselves — African Americans' continuing embrace and denial of their African past.

Wilson's focus as he rewrites and develops his work is revealed by comparing the successive drafts of each play. Cuts and extensions in the texts, the addition and elimination of characters, and altered action and endings all change the tone and theatrical effectiveness of the plays. All of the plays change significantly during the course of their development. *Ma Rainey's Black Bottom* did not include the band members in the first draft; *Joe Turner's Come and Gone* started as disconnected notes about a painting; in its first draft, it ran five and one-half hours. Wilson works quickly; he can write a play in only two months. But then he may take several years to rewrite the same play.

It is in Wilson's original act of creation where the collage methodology of Romare Bearden, his spiritual mentor, is recognizable. For months, even years, before he writes a play, he assembles its bits and pieces in various surroundings. Wilson thinks best in busy, noisy coffee shops, moving from one to another, ordering java and awaiting inspiration. Amid the crowd and noise, men and women he does not know fill his imagination with the stories of their lives; Wilson gathers bits of dialogue, sometimes writing them on small scraps of paper or napkins, and reciting them later to friends, refining and extending them as he goes. It

is the language of his characters, in whose truthfulness he believes
absolutely, that is at the heart of all of Wilson's plays.

> I start with the characters' dialogue. Often, I don't know who's
> talking or what they're talking about. But I start with a single
> line of dialogue and the more they talk, the more I get to know
> the characters.

> I believe that whatever a character says is true. So I write down
> everything the character says—pages and pages. Then, the trick
> is weeding through all that and finding the story that is really
> buried in there. And sometimes you really have to dig. You have
> to discover the connection of all the characters to the story that
> you're writing, to the play. That's the fun part.[4]

Wilson begins, then, by scattering his characters across his page.
He may apply an image from a painting, e.g. a brooding man at a
table, or a girl sitting at a piano. Then he will look for connections
between his bits of dialogue and his images. The connection may
be drawn from incidents in African-American history—a Martin
Luther King rally or enslavement by the infamous Joe Turney—
and he may find words for those connections in the lyrics of
a blues song—"Joe Turner's Come and Gone" or "Two Trains
Running."[5] He may incorporate real-life events to place his dramas
more specifically in time: a well-remembered baseball game plays
on the radio during *Fences*; a famous Joe Louis fight is broadcast
during *Seven Guitars*.

Sometimes, Wilson draws from his own history. Although he
is not an autobiographical writer, elements of his life do
appear in the details of his plays. He may borrow names:
Zonia and Bynum in *Joe Turner* were the names of Wilson's
grandparents; Sara Legree in *Two Trains* bears the name of a
Christian missionary from the neighborhood in which Wilson
grew up. He may assign his characters traits he remembers from
people he knew: two Wilson characters who cannot read, Troy and
Levee, recall Wilson's uncle and an old friend, both of whom
were illiterate.

Once all the pieces have been assembled, Wilson begins the process of putting them into an effective dramatic structure. And this is done largely through experimentation — moving pieces of a scene around within the scene or to an entirely different part of the play, moving whole sections of a play from one act to another.

Imagine a first draft — scenes one through eight. In Wilson's second draft, scene two and scene six switch places, the fourth and seventh scenes switch places, and scene one moves to the end. Wilson hears his new version and is dissatisfied. Next draft: scenes six and seven switch places and scene three moves to the top of the play. This reorganization may continue through the life of the show.

It may seem, on the surface, a haphazard method, impractical for the creation of drama, which usually has a more linear structure in which A clearly leads to B which clearly leads to C and so forth. And Wilson's colleagues sometimes find such a trial-and-error approach to composition confusing and seemingly lacking in overall vision. But for Wilson, it is the natural and inevitable expression of an instinctual artist whose initial conception is not linear: certain stories and events must be included, but not in any specific order. Actions need not necessarily precede or follow one another. He builds his dramas piece by piece, experimenting with effect. Wilson's description of this process evokes the continuing bond he feels with Romare Bearden: "It's pasting and putting things together," he says, "collage." [6]

As Wilson repeatedly reworks his overall structure, he also stops to attend to detail. He returns to the characters with whom he started the process. He clarifies his themes through his ongoing effort to explore the internal life of the people onstage, continually reexamining their choices and ensuring their individuality. A musician in *Ma Rainey's Black Bottom* had conflicting qualities, Wilson noticed, and so he split one character into two. Wilson cuts nothing at this early stage, but occasionally reassigns dialogue and action in order to clarify, define, and differentiate the characters.

> In *Seven Guitars*, when I started out, I had a character talking
> about his mother dying. He's getting roses and stuff and then
> the guy sings the Lord's Prayer. Well, at some point in the
> process, I decided that it's actually a different character whose
> mother I want to be dying. He was this second character who was
> always talking about his mother. In every other scene he was
> telling about his mother — my mother this, my mother that, and
> my mother used to do his and my mother used to do that.
>
> It occurred to me that ultimately I had the wrong character
> grieving. So I moved all the references where the first guy was talk-
> ing about his mother, and gave them to this second character.[7]

Wilson will also rework dialogue line by line, even word by word,
in order to ensure consistency of character. He makes hundreds
of such changes during the course of developing his plays.

The result of this intensive work is the creation of characters
whom the audience finds powerful to witness and the actors experience as powerful to portray. Indeed, the responses of actors and
actresses who have performed in Wilson's plays are a remarkable
testament to the magnitude and honesty of his characters. For
Charles Dutton, a Wilson play is anything but work.

> It's always great to see what August's rewrites will be the next day.
> You know, what he comes up with next, to heighten or enhance
> the character or the character's situation. It was a wonderful
> process for an actor to be involved in. Because one day you're
> doing one thing and the next day it's cut; and the next day
> you're doing a transplant of something else, the next week
> you're going back to what was cut a week before and it is placed
> somewhere else. So it's a roller coaster ride, but you don't panic.
> Because everything you've been given or had changed or
> renewed, it's still delicious language. Delicious story-telling, you
> know. You want the words to sing out of your mouth.[8]

Roscoe Lee Brown, who performed in *Joe Turner's Come and Gone* and

Two Trains Running, lights up when he discusses Wilson's plays.

> Isn't it extraordinary writing? Having had the real good fortune
> to work in the theater with great poets and dramatists, I put
> August Wilson very high in that pantheon. I believe absolutely
> that he is every bit as good as O'Neill. He plumbs the psyche as
> surely as any of the great dramatists and he knows how to sum-
> mon up race memories that make you whole.[9]

Sometimes, Wilson's actors suggest revisions. Indeed, he has learned to incorporate feedback from many sources. Even in the early
stages of his work, he wants actors to speak his lines, directors to
stage his scenes, and audiences to tell him when they are con-
fused. He has continually sought out the company of theater
artists and organizations who devote their energies to developing
new work. His plays have had readings and productions at institutions dedicated to the refinement of new American drama.
Wilson's words were honed through long meetings at New
Dramatists in New York, staged readings at the Eugene O'Neill
Theater Center's National Playwrights Conference, premieres at
the Yale Repertory or Goodman Theatre, and a series of regional
productions in which the plays underwent significant change on
their way to Broadway.

Earlier in his career, as Wilson's plays moved from theater to
theater, he did most of his rewriting in preparation for and immediately following the individual runs of the shows. Now, he works
more extensively during the rehearsal process, often in response
to those who are involved in the rehearsals, as evidenced by his
work on the recent production of his play *Jitney.* He listens to questions, addresses problems, considers suggestions. Although it
would be difficult to assign a specific change to a specific individual, directors, actors, dramaturgs, professional critics, and lay
people have influenced all of the plays.

Many of Wilson's collaborators have been white; the theaters
where he has hung his hat have primarily been what he refers to
as "white theaters"—those for whom the production of a black
play is the exception and not the rule. Recently he has spoken

9

out, calling for more black theaters and denouncing the damage he feels is being done to the black community as white theaters strive for diversity in their repertoire and their audience. In the controversial speech he delivered in June 1996, at the annual conference of the Theatre Communications Group, Wilson said that white theater productions of black plays are deleterious to "our already debilitated communities."[10] Wilson differentiates between black artists who write for white audiences and those who write for black audiences, placing himself among the latter. But Wilson admits that his plays are likely to continue to be produced at white theaters, an inconsistency for which he has been criticized.

Controversial as his words may have been, Wilson energized his entire audience as he reminded them of the power of theater to inform, to heal, to uncover truth. He specifically feels that black theater can "reignite and reunite our people's positive energy for a political and social change that is reflective of our spiritual truths rather than our economic fallacies."[11] But it remains to be seen whether this can happen in an integrated theater or whether only black theaters producing black work can achieve this goal. And it further remains to be seen whether Wilson's commitment to the racial politics of drama will affect the future of his work.

August Wilson is a powerful presence in the American theater. His plays have shaped our present; his politics may shape our future. Studying his history, his inspiration, and his methodology deepens our appreciation of Wilson's drama and offers significant insight into the creative process of his playwriting.

August Arrives

A Brief Professional
Biography

August Wilson was born Frederick August Kittel in 1945, the fourth of six children. He is the son of Daisy Wilson, an African-American woman, and Frederick August Kittel, a white German baker who left the family when Wilson was young. Wilson grew up in "the Hill," an integrated section of a primarily African-American area in Pittsburgh, where he later set several of his plays.

Wilson is largely self-taught. He spent much of his early life in the library, in the literary company of Richard Wright, Langston Hughes, Ralph Ellison. He dropped out of public school at age fifteen, when he was unjustly accused of plagiarism.

After spending some time on the streets, he took a series of jobs — gardener, porter, sheet metal worker, and short-order cook in a coffee shop, all of which appear in his plays. When he was twenty, his sister paid him twenty dollars to write a term paper comparing Robert Frost and Carl Sandburg; it was his first "professional" writing experience. He bought a typewriter with the money.

"The first thing I wanted to type was my name," Wilson remembers; when he did, Frederick Kittell became "August Wilson." Consciously discarding his father's history for the lineage of the mother who raised him, the young writer looked at what he had typed out on the page and said to himself: "That's all right, man that's all right. Then I began to type my poems."[1]

By the early 1970s, Wilson had read a range of American poets from Baraka to John Berryman. He was also passing time at the Halfway Art Gallery in Pittsburgh, a hot spot of beat culture where jazz was played at night and poetry read on Sundays. With a few friends, Wilson started the Centre Avenue Poets Theater Workshop which sponsored readings and published small poetry magazines. And two literary journals, *Black World* and *Black Lines*, began publishing Wilson's poetry. In 1969, Wilson wed Brenda Burton and although the marriage did not last, in 1970, his daughter, Sakina Ansari, was born.

Wilson's political interests led him to the theater. Working with playwright, professor, and friend Rob Penny, Wilson founded Black Horizon on the Hill, an African-American activist theater company, through which he hoped to politicize the community and raise consciousness. Initially, Wilson produced and directed the plays of Ed Bullins and other African-American writers. Soon he was inspired to try his own hand at playwriting.

Wilson's first play, which he can readily recite in its entirety, lacked a certain dramatic flair.

"What's happening?"
"Nothing."[2]

Undeterred by the brevity of this endeavor, Wilson wrote several one-act plays over the next three years, including *Recycle, The Janitor, The Homecoming,* and *The Coldest Day of the Year.* But Wilson was dissatisfied with these early efforts and continued to work mainly as a poet. In the mid 1970s, he gave a reading of a long poem entitled *Black Bart and the Sacred Hills,* the story of a stagecoach robber in the old West. When Claude Purdy, a friend of Wilson's who was a theater director, heard the reading, he urged him to turn the poem into a play. It took the new playwright four months to complete the 120-page musical satire, complete with six songs he wrote himself.

Black Bart was first presented as a staged reading at the Inner City Cultural Center in Los Angeles. As written, the play ran over five hours, but the project's director cut the work to under one hour before its presentation without discussing the changes with Wilson. This first experience as a "produced" playwright left a bitter taste in his mouth.

Nonetheless, Wilson sent *Black Bart* to Claude Purdy, who had moved to St. Paul, Minnesota, to become the director of Penumbra, an African-American theater. In November of 1977, Purdy invited Wilson to St. Paul to rewrite the play. Purdy then mounted a production at his theater. With its large cast and rambling structure, *Black Bart* was cumbersome and Wilson did not seek further productions.

Wilson preferred St. Paul to his native Pittsburgh and decided to stay on there. For two years, he worked at the Science Museum in nearby Minneapolis, writing the dialogue that accompanied diorama exhibits. Then, an actress friend invited him to hear a reading of a new play. Despite his own inexperience, Wilson was "unimpressed."

> I went to see it and I thought, well I can write a better play than this. So I kind of filed that away in my head and resolved myself that I would write a better play.[3]

But Wilson was wary, concerned, as he reviewed his earlier work, about his ability to create effective voices for his characters. Although today his extraordinary dialogue inspires his audiences who consistently murmur "That's right," or "Tell it" during his plays, Wilson knew his first efforts were inadequate:

> The dialogue wasn't good. I couldn't write plays because I couldn't write dialogue. I asked a friend of mine [director Rob Penny], "How do you make them talk," and he said, "You don't make them talk—you listen to them." And I realized my mistake. I was trying to force words into their mouths instead of listening and not only listening but recognizing the poetry that was inherent in the way black people spoke."[4]

Ultimately, Wilson began to listen to the voices in his neighbor-

13

hood and even admits to stealing, for later use, what he terms "authentic" dialogue from the old men who frequented Pat's cigar shop on the corner. His confidence in his newfound ear for dialogue, combined with the lingering self-challenge to write a "better play," encouraged him to create *Jitney* in 1979.

Jitney, a realistic drama set in a gypsy cab station in Pittsburgh, represented a significant step in the development of Wilson's dramaturgy. Set in a neighborhood in which he had lived, it was the first of Wilson's plays to use realistic dialogue and it was far more complex in its attempt to intertwine the stories of its independent characters. When Wilson submitted *Jitney* to the Playwrights Center in St. Paul, he won a Jerome Fellowship, which included a small stipend; for the first time, he began to think of himself as a playwright.

> When I went to the Playwright's Center and I sat in the room and there were sixteen playwrights in the room I thought I must be a playwright cause I'm sitting here with these other sixteen playwrights. And it was important for me to start to think of myself as a playwright. Claiming it and thinking of myself as a playwright enabled me to do the work. And my creative energy, that unnamed, unformed thing, that for me previously went toward poetry now began to siphon off and began to go into theater, into playwriting. [5]

Wilson quit his full-time job at the Science Museum. Working half days as a cook for a social service organization, The Little Brothers of the Poor, he wrote the rest of the day. Wilson's next play was *Fullerton Street*. Set in 1941, the play examines the clash between rural Southern and urban Northern values. But with twenty-seven characters, the play is large and unwieldy, and Wilson eventually decided not to allow it to be produced.

In 1980, Wilson submitted *Fullerton Street* and *Jitney* to the Eugene O'Neill Theater Center's National Playwrights Conference in Waterford, Connecticut, one of the country's leading bastions for the development of new plays. They sent them back. Convinced that they had not read the work, Wilson resubmitted the plays the following year. Again, they sent them back. Wilson reconsidered his position.

> When they sent them back to me the second time I said maybe they're not as good as I think. So I told myself, well you've got to write a better play, if you want to go to the O'Neill. And I asked myself how do I do that because I was already writing the best play that I can write. And that's when I decided to up my sights, so to speak. Instead of writing a play just to get to the O'Neill, I thought, well, I would write the best play that's ever been written. And then I would go to the O'Neill, of course, if it's the best play that's ever been written. And that's when I wrote *Ma Rainey's Black Bottom.*[6]

But even while Wilson was writing *Ma Rainey*, early in 1982, *Jitney* was being produced at Pittsburgh's Allegheny Repertory Theater with tremendous success, selling out every night. Many audience members, African Americans attending the theater for the first time, refused to leave when the play was over.[7] But it was the success of *Ma Rainey* that would bring Wilson national attention and change his artistic life.

A drama about exploitation and the consequences of the tolerance of injustice, *Ma Rainey's Black Bottom* centers on the legendary blues singer Ma Rainey and the musicians in her band. This powerful play was accepted for the 1982 O'Neill Conference. The following spring, Lloyd Richards, then the Artistic Director of the Conference, as well as the Artistic Director of the Yale Repertory Theatre, in New Haven, Connecticut, scheduled *Ma Rainey's Black Bottom* for production at Yale Rep. Wilson continued to work on the play before its production and then, after attending over forty performances, he made many changes before the play moved on. Following its run in New Haven, the play ran briefly at the Annenberg Center in Philadelphia and then moved to Broadway in October 1984. Wilson had to borrow a tuxedo for the opening.

Anxious to prove his productivity, Wilson began his next play even before *Ma Rainey* had its first full production at Yale Rep.

Fences, set in the 1950s, focuses on Troy Maxson, a disappointed former baseball player whose career ended before African-American men were allowed to play professional baseball outside of the Negro Leagues. Troy's disappointments and his efforts to prove his manhood ultimately cause the disintegration of his family.

In July 1983, *Fences* was developed at the O'Neill Conference. In April 1985, it opened at the Yale Repertory Theatre, again under the direction of Lloyd Richards. Later that year, the production moved to the Goodman Theatre in Chicago. *Fences* then played in Seattle and San Francisco, and it opened at the 46th Street Theater on Broadway in March of 1987. *Fences* won the New York Drama Critics Circle Award for Best Play, four Tony Awards, and the Pulitzer Prize for Drama.

Fences was still playing on Broadway when Wilson's next play, *Joe Turner's Come and Gone*, opened one year later. *Joe Turner* began its development at New Dramatists in New York City, the nation's oldest non-profit workshop for playwrights. New Dramatists was founded in 1949 and continues to pursue its original goal — its dedication "to finding gifted playwrights and giving them the time, the space, and the tools to develop their craft, so that they can reach their full potential and make lasting contributions to the American theater."[8]

Wilson was invited to join New Dramatists in 1984, where in the spring, the organization sponsored a staged reading of *Mill Hand's Lunch Bucket* (the original title of *Joe Turner*), followed by a panel discussion. Wilson was excited to hear his work early in its life.

> It was an opportunity to test what worked and what didn't work. There are a lot of things you can't evaluate until you see it staged. You could read it over and over again and still not tell. You can write a short story on your own but not a play.[9]

Wilson then brought his play to the O'Neill Conference and it opened at the Yale Rep in May 1986, once again under the direction of Lloyd Richards. Following productions at the Huntington Theater Company in Boston, the Seattle Repertory Theater, the Arena Stage in Washington, D.C., and the Old Globe in San Diego, the play opened on Broadway in March of 1988.

Set in Pittsburgh, in 1911, *Joe Turner* addresses the feelings of loss and spiritual confusion experienced by African Americans in the post-Emancipation period. The play explores issues which would become central to Wilson's work.

> When black Americans emigrated from the South to the North they lost certain connections — connections I think we as black Americans need to go back and make. For 200 years we developed a culture in the South and when we moved north we abandoned that and lost our tie to our history. Kids today do not know who they are because they have no connection to their grandparents and no connection with their political history in America.[10]

The need to reckon with a tragic past also permeates Wilson's next play. In *The Piano Lesson*, set in the 1930s, Boy Willie and his sister Berniece grapple over a piano which bears images of family members carved by their enslaved ancestors. At issue is whether to keep or sell this family heirloom and ultimately whether to accept or deny the past. *The Piano Lesson* followed the same route as Wilson's other works, arriving on Broadway in April of 1990, and winning him a second Pulitzer Prize for Drama. Wilson was the sixth playwright to achieve this honor twice.[11]

As *The Piano Lesson* was opening on Broadway, *Two Trains Running* was opening at the Yale Repertory Theatre. *Two Trains Running* is set in 1969 in a local diner where its characters are buffeted by the turbulent sixties as the play explores issues of economic and spiritual empowerment and the impact of collective action. *Two Trains Running*, directed by Lloyd Richards, traveled a short regional circuit on its way to Broadway where it opened in 1991.

Perhaps in homage to Romare Bearden's continuing inclusion of musicians, Wilson first titled his newest play *Guitar Serenade* but came to prefer *Seven Guitars*. Floyd Barton pursues the road to great musical success, encumbered by a woman unforgiving of his wanderings, a manager arrested for insurance fraud, and a distinct lack of cash. But it is battle with the forces of fate, an unusual twist of events, and the rage of a man long denied what the world owes to him that ultimately deny Floyd his dream and his life.

In January, 1995, *Seven Guitars* opened at the Goodman Theatre in Chicago. Lloyd Richards, now retired from the artistic directorship of the Yale Rep, was set to direct the world premiere. Before rehearsals began, however, Richards became ill and was replaced by Walter Dallas. The production received primarily positive reviews and set out on what had become the traditional Wilson route. Richards rejoined the production as it made its way from one regional theater to another and eventually to Broadway.

Despite the frequent arrival of new work by Wilson, his older plays remain popular and are continually produced. Even his early work has attracted interest. Wilson's belief that "they always remembered *Jitney* in Pittsburgh," was reaffirmed when The Pittsburgh Public Theater produced *Jitney* in June 1996. Wilson rewrote extensively for this and the following production at The Crossroads Theatre in New Brunswick, N.J. The production by a now-veteran playwright received far more exposure than it had in 1979.

But Wilson's focus is on the future and he plans to write a play for each decade of this century providing a sustained dramatic embodiment of the African-American experience. He describes it as "the dramatic tracing of the black American odyssey."[12] To date, Wilson has covered seventy years. He works continually, pressuring himself to have a play in progress at all times. No amount of accolade seems able to give him a feeling of artistic security.

> All those awards, all that stuff, I take them and I hang them on my wall. But then I turn around and my typewriter's sitting there, and it doesn't know from awards. I always tell people I'm a struggling playwright. I'm struggling to get the next play down on paper. You start at the beginning each time you sit down. Nothing you've written before has any bearing on what you're going to write now. It's like a heavyweight fighter. You've gotta go and knock the guy out. It doesn't matter if you're undefeated.

18

There's another guy standing there, and you have to go out
again, and you have to duck his punches and do all the rest of
whatever it is you do.[13]

Although Wilson actively resisted work in film for several years, he
has recently taken the plunge. In 1987, Paramount Pictures,
encouraged by Eddie Murphy, purchased the film rights to *Fences*
and hired Wilson to write the screenplay. But film production was
halted when Wilson clashed with the studio. He insisted on an
African-American director: "What I thought of as a straightfor-
ward, logical request," he wrote, "has been greeted by blank,
vacant stares and the pious shaking of heads as if in response to
my unfortunate naivete."[14] The debate garnered significant press
and eventually the project became too controversial to pursue.

Wilson then adapted *The Piano Lesson* for the small screen. It
was produced by Hallmark Hall of Fame, directed by Lloyd
Richards, and premiered on network television in the spring
of 1995. Wilson is constantly pursued by Hollywood executives
anxious for the prestige of an association with a Pulitzer Prize-
winning author. But he will not allow his screenplays to be
rewritten by other writers prior to production, which is
Hollywood's modus operandi, and so the wary studios usually
shy away from making a deal.

Wilson now lives in Seattle with his wife Constanza Romera
and their daughter, Azula, born in 1997; he moved there in an
effort to escape the bitter cold of St. Paul. Now, it is the rain that
keeps him indoors and writing. But Wilson returns often to his
native Pittsburgh and the Hill district. He enjoys walking the
streets of his old neighborhood, greeting the people about whom
he writes and listening to their voices.

The Four "B's"

August Wilson's Inspiration

It is often difficult to discover an artist's muse. But in naming his four "B's," Wilson points toward his creative spark and leads his critics straight to the visual and aural images that inspire him. Wilson starts with the image—the image that will appear within the play and that will be central to the play's resolution. Then, he moves back in time to create the story, filling a blank sheet of paper with the words of rich and complex characters until he arrives at the moment when the image is fully explained and captured.

Images on canvas, collage/paintings by the artist Romare Bearden, have directly inspired three of Wilson's plays. Wilson first saw *Continuities*, a painting of a large man holding a small baby, in a book of Bearden's work. The image stuck, and years later it appeared in the pivotal scene of *Fences*. In the play, Troy Maxson has an affair which produces a child. When the infant's mother dies in childbirth, Troy brings the baby home, hoping his wife will care for her.

> A man's got to do what's right for him. I ain't sorry for nothing
> I done. It felt right in my heart....She's my daughter, Rose. My
> own flesh and blood...I can't deny her no more than I can deny

them boys. You and them boys is my family. You and them and this child is all I got in the world. So I guess what I'm saying is...I'd appreciate it if you'd help me take care of her.[1]

As he stands in his yard with his newborn daughter in his arms, the moment is a triumph, not just as drama, but because Wilson achieved what he set out to do after first being exposed to Bearden's work.

What I saw was black life presented on its own terms, on a grand and epic scale, with all its richness and fullness, in a language that was vibrant and which, made attendant to everyday life, ennobled it, affirmed its value, and exalted its presence. In Bearden I found my artistic mentor and sought, and still aspire, to make my plays the equal of his canvasses.[2]

Bearden's *The Piano Lesson* had an even more immediate impact on Wilson. The moment he encountered the silk screen in an art gallery, Wilson turned to a friend and said, "This will be my next play."[3] The silk screen depicts a woman instructing a child at the piano. In the course of developing the story behind this image, Wilson provided a rich history. The drama of *The Piano Lesson* focuses on a struggle between Boy Willie, and his sister Berniece, over whether to sell the piano they have inherited: Boy Willie wants the money to buy land; Berniece wants to keep the heirloom.

The instrument had previously been owned by the Sutter family, who had enslaved Boy Willie's and Berniece's parents and grandparents. The slave owner acquired the piano in a trade — the musical instrument for Berniece and Boy Willie's father and grandmother. Grieving for his wife and child who were taken from him, the grandfather of Berniece and Boy Willie carved portraits of his family into the wooden legs. Years later his son, Berniece and Boy Willie's father, lost his life reclaiming the piano.

Unwilling as she is to part with it, Berniece is also unwilling to play the piano; she fears that to do so would raise the spirits embodied within it. But, as in the image Wilson took from Bearden's painting, she is teaching her daughter Maretha to play, and eventually she is forced to call forth the spirits to empower and save her brother as he wrestles with Sutter's ghost. Boy Willie then agrees that Berniece can keep the piano, on one condition: "If you and Maretha don't keep playing on that piano...ain't no telling...me and Sutter both liable to be back."[4] He, too, is true to that original image from the painting.

In a third Wilson play directly inspired by Bearden, both art and artist provided raw material. Wilson first saw Bearden's 1978 work, *Mill Hand's Lunch Bucket*, in a magazine. *Mill Hand* reflected the childhood years Bearden spent at his maternal grandmother's boarding house in Pittsburgh. The collage shows a busy household as its inhabitants prepare for their day.

Mill Hand's Lunch Bucket fascinated Wilson, who was particularly drawn to the haunting and lonely figure who sat at its center. "He was sitting in the middle of all these people. But all the people are going out and soon he's going to be by himself."[5] When Wilson first saw the painting, he himself was working on a series of poems entitled "Restoring the House" which followed the path of a freed slave as he searched for his wife who had been sold to another plantation owner five years before Emancipation. Breathing life into the dark and mysterious figure at the center of Bearden's collage, and providing him a past inspired by the action of "Restoring the House," Wilson created Herald Loomis, the central figure in *Joe Turner's Come and Gone*.

Loomis is a man who was separated from his wife when the infamous Joe Turner forced him into servitude. In order to draw the characters closer to the time of slavery, Wilson set his play in 1911, about ten or twelve years earlier than the time in which Bearden's art work is set. Because the earlier time frame was inconsistent with the steel mills suggested by Bearden's collage, the men in Wilson's boarding house work on the road instead of in an industrial setting. But in making that substitution, Wilson was careful to choose a form of work equally integral to the experience of African Americans during their northward migration.

Wilson schooled himself in Bearden's life as well as his art, borrowing images from both. The physical set Wilson specified for *Joe Turner's Come and Gone* closely resembles the sketches Bearden made of his grandmother's Pittsburgh boarding house. Wilson even went so far as to create a young character he names Reuben, who is a representation of Bearden himself as a boy. In the mid 1920s, the young Bearden befriended a sickly child named Eugene who collected pigeons. Eugene made Bearden promise to free the birds when he died, an event which followed shortly. In Wilson's play, young Reuben explains to Loomis' daughter Zonia that the pigeons he keeps were left to him by his friend, Eugene, who died recently. Reuben was supposed to have freed them, but he hasn't had the heart to give up the birds. Late in the play, Reuben dreams of a ghost who inspires him to open the coop.

The collage technique Bearden uses in much of his best known work had as much of an impact on Wilson as did the images themselves. In his collages, Bearden used a variety of found objects, creating a relationship among them as they were assembled. He thought of his work as play—not child's play but "a kind of divine play" in which he took found objects, e.g. cloth, photographs, pieces of wood, and arranged and rearranged them until he had produced an effective image.

Wilson was intrigued by Bearden's ability to collect images that are individually significant within African-American culture and to increase their resonance through the juxtaposition of one with another. He was particularly interested in Bearden's incorporation of traditional African elements into contemporary art. For example, Bearden combines African masks with African-American faces cut out from modern magazines, thus illuminating the process of African Americans trying to meld past and future, to find their place in time, their identity.

This use of juxtaposed imagery hit home with Wilson who believes that "In a world dominated by white culture, the black must be strong enough not only to survive but to reestablish his own identity and heritage which flows unbroken from an African fountainhead."[6] Inspired by Bearden, Wilson's drama promotes an understanding of how the African culture of their past can continue to speak to African Americans. For example, the characters in *Joe Turner* perform a juba, a call-and-response dance "reminiscent of the ring shouts of the African slaves."[7] And the word "Juba" itself is West African for "ancestors."

Following Bearden's lead, Wilson builds his plays from small pieces drawn from a wide variety of sources, including history. However, he does not study the historical periods about which he writes; rather he allows the bits of history he remembers to float into his mind, thence into the work, wherever they seem to suit the dramatic needs of his overall structure.

To bits of history, pieces of their own lives, and people created in their minds, Wilson and Bearden add images pulled from a shared pool. They are simple images and symbols but endowed with great significance. Of the common images which weave through the two artists' works, trains are perhaps the most important. Bearden explains that "trains are so much a part of Negro life. Negroes lived near the tracks, worked on the railroads and trains carried them North during the migration."[8] They recur in many of Bearden's works, appearing either centrally (*The Train*), or in the background (*Southern Limited*).

Bearden's frequent use of trains in his work catalyzed Wilson's own recognition of the importance of trains in African-American history. *Two Trains Running* acknowledges that centrality. In the play, the character Memphis speaks about returning to his home in the south. But knowing "what they do to a nigger they see driving a Cadillac," Memphis plans on taking the train: "They got two trains running every day."[9] Wilson's early play, *The Homecoming*, is reminiscent of Bearden's painting *Watching the Trains Go By* (1964). The central image in both is a small train station where two men wait.

The guitar is another important image for both Wilson and Bearden. This instrument appears in many Bearden collage paintings, including *Blues at the Crossroads*, *The Street*, and *The Guitar Player*, and also figures prominently in several of Wilson's plays, including *The Homecoming* and *Joe Turner's Come and Gone* in which the character of Jeremy, who has brought only his guitar with him from the South, makes it the instrument of a profitable livelihood.

Guitar players specifically and music more generally find their way into the work of these two artists as both technique and subject. Wilson sees "Bearden's use of the collage...[as] the visual equivalent of rapping and blues—music that you sort of have to piece together as it jumps from one thing to the next."[10] Wilson, too, likes to use improvisation in his creative process to experiment with multiple variations on a single theme. Like the musical forms and images which inspire them, Wilson's plays are metaphorical, lyrical, and loosely organized. Listening to Wilson's dialogue, one hears the repartee of jazz in the carefully orchestrated quick exchanges of dialogue, the soulfulness of the blues in the long speeches of the characters.

The blues stand as Wilson's most profound reference tool. "Anything you want to know about the black experience is in the blues," Wilson says. "The blues is The Book—it is our sacred book."[11]

The little-acknowledged contribution of African Americans to the music industry is one of Wilson's central themes. He dedicated his early one-act play, *The Homecoming*, to "the memory of Blind singers whose story remains largely untold."[12] The action of the play occurs while two friends of the fictional blues singer Blind Willie, Leroy and Obadiah, await the return of his dead body by train. Obadiah tells how he died:

> He was doing right nice for a while too. Shucks, he'd sing four songs and make him a hundred dollars...And after he sing all his songs...they didn't need him no more. Nossir. They had his voice trapped in one of them fancy recording machines and they could hear him sing anytime they wanted to... then they put him out of that fancy hotel. Made like they never seen him before. Called the police on him when he went down to their office to get his money he made on them records they was selling all over Harlem...Blind Willie starved to death...That's right. Froze to death on somebody's doorstep.[13]

Leroy and Obadiah kill the two white record producers who spot them at the train station and approach them. Looking for any "coon with a guitar," the producers hope to make a fast buck off

Leroy and Obadiah. But with the help of Blind Willie's son, the two friends cripple the white men and seal them in the station as revenge for the death of Blind Willie. The play is accompanied by Blind Lemon Jefferson's recording of "Bad Luck Blues."

> I wanna go home and I ain't got sufficient clothes
> (doggone my bad luck soul)
> Wanna go home and I ain't got sufficient clothes
> I mean sufficient cold weather clothes
> Well I wanna go home and I ain't got sufficient clothes.[14]

Wilson also includes the lyrics of Blind Lemon Jefferson on the first page of his published version of *Ma Rainey's Black Bottom*.

> They tore the railroad down
> So the Sunshine Special can't run
> I'm going away baby
> Build me a railroad of my own[15]

Certainly Wilson's most directly blues-inspired play is *Ma Rainey's Black Bottom*, for which the music provides title, central character, theme, and action. The real-life Ma Rainey, nee Gertrude Pridgett, began her career as a minstrel artist, performing with her husband as Ma and Pa Rainey. The couple was known for their singing and dancing, particularly a number called "The Black Bottom." But Wilson did not know much of Ma Rainey's history when he began his play in 1976. He was driven by the emotional content of her recordings and the power of her performance, and was drawn to her as an icon, much as he had been galvanized by the people in the Bearden paintings.

So Wilson began with the image of Ma Rainey, the blues queen, her arms outstretched, surrounded by her entourage, a scene that stood in stark contrast to the day-to-day realities of her life as a typically-exploited black artist, working in an industry known for its blatant disregard for its performers. Ma reflects, "As soon as they get my voice down on them recording machines, then it's just like I'd be some whore and they roll over and put their pants on. Ain't got no use for me then. I know what I'm talking about."[16]

Wilson's familiarity with a variety of blues music and his appreciation of the blues' vitality in the African-American experience encouraged him to integrate music throughout *Ma Rainey's Black Bottom*. At the end of Act I, the character of Levee tells the horrifying story of the rape of his mother by eight white men and the hanging of his father who tried to avenge the crime. There is a long pause when Levee concludes. Then, Slow Drag begins playing on his bass and sings.

> If I had my way
> If I had my way
> If I had my way
> I would tear this old building down.[17]

Wilson pulled his image of the bluesman from the history of the music. A descendent of the *griote*, an African story teller, the bluesman's role was to voice the truths, ironies, joys, heartbreak, and suppressed anger of the community.

Wilson also understands the ways in which people use the blues as comfort and solace. As Ma waits to begin recording "Black Bottom," she sings to herself, relieving her physical pain but, more significantly, her mental pain.

> Oh Lord, these dogs of mine
> They sure do worry me all the time
> The reason why I don't know
> Lord, I best to be excused
> I can't wear me no sharp-toed shoes
> I went for a walk
> I stopped to talk
> Oh how my corns did bark.[18]

In almost every Wilson play, a character sings the blues to replenish his or her spirit. In *Seven Guitars*, Louise sings a bawdy song for what Wilson's stage direction describes as a "much needed affirmation of life:"

> Anybody here wanna try good cabbage
> just step this way
> Anybody here like to try good cabbage
> just holler hey
>
> I gave some to the parson
> and he shook with glee
> He took up a collection
> and gave it all to me
> Anybody here wanna try good cabbage
> just step this way.[19]

In *The Piano Lesson*, as Boy Willie's Uncle Doaker irons, he sings a song he learned while working on the railroad. Wilson writes in a stage direction that the song provides a rhythm for Doaker's work and makes the chore less burdensome. Combining images again, Wilson has given a voice to Bearden's trainman.

The blues are also sung by Boy Willie's other uncle, Wining Boy, a gambler and musician. Wining Boy has had a troubled life and his music reflects his complaints.

> Tell me how long
> Is I got to wait
> Can I get it now
> Or must I hesitate
>
> It take a hesitating stocking her hesitating shoe
> It takes a hesitating woman wanna sing the blues
>
> Tell me how long
> Is I got to wait
> Can I kiss you now
> Or must I hesitate.[20]

28

Joe Turner's Come and Gone, which had originally been titled *Mill Hand's Lunch Bucket* after Bearden's painting, took its name from an old blues song. It was a song sung at the turn of the century by the women left behind when the legendary Joe Turney, brother of the governor of Tennessee, collected African-American men to intern for seven years of labor.

> They tell me Joe Turner's come and gone
> Ohhh Lordy
> They tell me Joe Turner's come and gone
> Got my man and gone.
>
> Come with forty links of chain
> Ohhh Lordy,
> Come with forty links of chain
> Ohhh Lordy,
> Got my man and gone.[21]

In this simple verse, Wilson found his own version of what was haunting the solitary figure in Bearden's painting.

The old blues song is sung once in the play, not by Herald Loomis, but by the character Bynum, who has heard it sung by the women in the fields near Memphis. Bynum sings it because he recognizes that Loomis is lost. Unable to acknowledge the slavery of his own past, Loomis has severed his cultural connection to his ancestors. Bynum sings to challenge Loomis to remember, reflecting Wilson's faith in the healing power of the blues.

Another kind of blues makes an appearance in *The Piano Lesson.* Boy Willie and his friend Lymon have come up North, to the home of Boy Willie's sister, Berniece, to retrieve Boy Willie's family piano. As they relax, Boy Willie and Lymon remember the trouble they have left behind in the South and the days they spent on the Parchman work farm. Part and parcel of their memory are the songs they sang to ease their load.

> Go 'head marry don't you wait on me oh-ah
> Go 'head marry don't you wait on me oh-ah

> Might not want you when I go free oh-ah
> Might not want you when I go free well
>
> O Lord Berta Berta O Lord gal oh-ah
> O Lord Berta Berta O Lord gal well
>
> Berta in Meridan and she living at ease oh-ah
> Berta in Meridan and she living at ease well
> I'm on old Parchman, got to work or leave oh-ah
> I'm on old Parchman, got to work or leave well.[22]

Boy Willie and Lymon, joined by Boy Willie's uncles, stomp their feet and clap to keep time. "Oh Berta" is a typical Mississippi Valley work-gang song, sung by hundreds of men as they worked in the fields or cleared the land.

Like the songs, Wilson's plays speak of disappointment. They include stories of unfulfilled dreams, crushing oppression, and personal defeat. But like the blues, the plays are full of energy and life. Wilson strove to make his plays equal to the music in their ability "to capture the core of black life and to stand as a testament to the resiliency of the human spirit."[23]

Wilson's guide in translating his vision to the stage was Amiri Baraka who wrote of his own efforts, "We wanted art that would actually reflect black life and its history and its legacy of resistance and struggle. We wanted art as black as our music."[24]

Baraka (nee Everett Leroy Jones) was at the height of his playwriting career when Wilson first ventured into the theater. Inspired by the forms and themes of the veteran playwright, Wilson started by following in his stylistic footsteps. Indeed, Wilson's first plays reveal his experimentation with several styles in which Baraka wrote. Wilson's *Black Bart and the Sacred Hills* is a wild satire that takes its form from Baraka's *Great Goodness Life: The Coon Show*. Wilson had seen *Great Goodness Life* performed by Baraka's troupe at a loft in Harlem and was energized.

> It's wild and zany and it is extremely effective. Baraka takes his anger and makes art out of it. It's funny and it gets his point

across. Baraka wanted to make everything big. And I thought
that this was one of the ways that he was most effective. Very theatrical — sometimes I couldn't understand drama but I understood theatrics. It's truly art.[25]

Black Bart, a complex musical set in the old west, is Wilson's only
attempt at this form.

As Wilson continued his career in playwriting in the early
1970s, Baraka was writing his most revolutionary drama. *Home on
the Range, The Death of Malcolm X, Arm Yourself or Harm Yourself,
Junkies Are Full of SHHH...,* and *Police* are all short, angry plays, theater intended to "accuse and attack."[26] These plays are far from
the theater for which Wilson is known, but, at the time, Wilson
shared Baraka's politics and followed his lead in writing the politically revolutionary one-act play, *The Homecoming.* At the play's
close, Blind Willie's son, Will Jr., comes out of the train station
with a shotgun. When Obadiah asks if these are the same men
who exploited Blind Willie, Leroy replies: "It don't matter. I can't
tell for sure. You know something, Obadiah...it's the funniest
thing...I can't figure it out...but they all look alike to me."[27] At
Leroy's direction, Will Jr. herds the two white men into the train
station. Because Will Jr. is short on bullets, Leroy breaks the
men's backs and then he and Obadiah seal them in the station.
Like Baraka's work, Wilson's play promotes an act of violence as
vengeance for exploitation

In their exploration of oppression and the appropriate
response to it, Wilson's plays follow an opposite pattern from that
of Baraka. Having started with his most revolutionary "accuse
and attack" play, Wilson then moved toward Baraka's earlier
explorations of internal conflict within his characters. Thus, the
focus of *Ma Rainey's Black Bottom* is very different from that of *The
Homecoming. Ma Rainey* also examines the exploitation of African-
American blues musicians, and the figure of the oppressive record
producer, now Sturdyvant, reappears in this play. But in *Ma
Rainey,* Levee does not kill Sturdyvant; Wilson rejects an external
solution to exploitation and instead focuses on the change Levee
must make within himself in order to survive.

Levee is a musician in Ma's band but he wants his own recording contract and he will do anything to get it. His desires breed conflict as he tries to deny his cultural past in order to secure his musical future. Wilson reveals the confusion and impotence that result from Levee's tolerance of exploitation and from his desire to succeed within the white man's world.

The theme picks up on Baraka's early work, which portrayed characters whose desire to integrate into white society promotes self-destruction. Wilson's Levee is reminiscent of the character of Clay in Baraka's early play *Dutchman*. Clay, an African-American man, encounters Lula, a white woman, in a subway car. They flirt, they argue, and eventually, she stabs him.

The play's external violence is the result of Clay's internal conflict. It is a conflict shared by Levee: the simultaneous attraction to what white culture has to offer and the need to rebel against it— the choice between assimilation and revolution. At first, Clay fulfills Lula's stereotypic expectations of his behavior. He panders to Lula's advances. But then he erupts into a furious attack on her racist view of him:

> You don't know anything except what's there for you to see. An act. Lies. Device. Not the pure heart, the pumping black heart. You don't ever know that. And I sit here, in this buttoned-up suit, to keep myself from cutting all your throats. I mean wantonly.[28]

Levee follows this model, alternating between acts of ingratiation and aggression. First he shuffles (as his fellow band members describe it) when the white record producer enters the room. Then, when Sturdyvant leaves, he talks of violence, professing his readiness to stab him in the back. Ultimately, Baraka's figure, Clay, rejects the option of revolution and dies doing so, while Levee's choices culminate in a much more complex kind of violence. In *Ma Rainey's Black Bottom*, the violence does not occur between oppressor and victim; in response to Sturdyvant's devastating refusal to record Levee's music, Levee stabs his fellow band member, Toledo. Reflecting the changed political climate provided by the nearly twenty year span between the writing of these two plays, Wilson has moved from an inter-community conflict to an intra-community conflict, one with greater resonance for contemporary audiences.

Wilson's focus, then, is on more psychologically complex characters. They face a kind of oppression that is comprised of external and internal forces. The characters in Wilson's plays are struggling to define themselves as individuals and to understand their place in the world. It is only through internal change that they can successfully face external affliction.

Although the experiences Wilson writes about in his plays may be specific to the African-American community at certain points in time and place, the characters he portrays and the personal drama they live out are familiar to people of many colors, as evidenced by Wilson's commercial success. The relevance of these characters to contemporary audiences and their cross-cultural recognizability make them a significant departure from the kind of characters Baraka was creating in his revolutionary plays of the late sixties and early seventies. But Wilson still found inspiration in Baraka's work and says, "What I tried to do was follow him by doing not necessarily the work he did, but the kind of work I thought he was calling for: work that would, in essence, expose the culture and demonstrate its vitality and its ability to sustain you."[29]

In portraying his culture and prescribing for its future, Wilson, like Baraka, promotes self-definition, self-determination, and cultural nationalism even at the possible cost of exclusion from the American dream. Wilson's work is a call for African Americans to build their future from the building blocks of their own culture and not from materials borrowed from the white culture. "The sign on America's door is leave your Africanness outside. My sign says claim what is yours."[30]

For example, like Baraka, Wilson questions African-American acceptance of traditional Christian doctrine. In Baraka's play *The Baptism*, set in a church, a young boy is accused of masturbating while praying. In an effort to reclaim the boy, a minister and an old woman come into conflict with a homosexual, a man cast out by the church but, in fact, as Baraka makes clear, the character who is closest to God. Baraka sees the Christian church as hypocritically false and even evil.

Wilson explored this theme in preliminary drafts of several plays. In an early version of *Ma Rainey's Black Bottom*, the musician Toledo explains why he left the church.

> I done read the bible, all about Jacob and all the things he done went and done wrong and all the time God whispering in his ear and ain't chastise him for his evil doing...and I done decided that the god of Jacob ain't none of my God.[31]

In an early version of *Fences*, Troy Maxim yells to God, wondering why He hasn't kept His end of the deal:

> I done give you everything you asked for. I don't have no other gods before you...I don't lie...I don't steal...I keep hold the Sabbath...I don't covet my neighbors goods...I done give you everything! I done paid up on the dues but where's my benefits? I ain't strode through the waters of Jordan for nothing! I ain't walked through the Valley of the shadow of Death to find nothing on the other side! I ain't turned my cheek to the hands of my enemies to be struck down?[32]

But Wilson eventually cut this material as he moved from a general condemnation of an unjust, hypocritical God, indeed one whose ways have been questioned by men of all colors, to a more specific condemnation of the neglect of African Americans by the white man's God. "Of all the people in the world, only black Americans have a God who doesn't resemble them. And they want so badly to assimilate, they can't even see they're worshiping some one else's God."[33] This view is reflected in *Ma Rainey's Black Bottom*, when Cutler tells the story of the life-threatening humiliation of an African-American minister by several white men. Levee offers a blistering response:

> Why didn't God strike some of them crackers down? Tell me that! That's the question! Don't come telling me this burning-in-hell shit! He a man of God...Why didn't God strike some of them crackers down? I'll tell you why!...'Cause he's a white

man's God...God ain't never listened to no nigger's prayers.[34]

Moving far beyond Baraka's simpler depictions of Christian hypocrisy, *Joe Turner's Come and Gone* contains Wilson's scathing indictment of Jesus Christ himself. When Martha Pentacost recites the Lord's Prayer in an effort to save her husband, Herald Loomis responds:

> You can't tell me nothing about no valleys. I done been all across the valleys and the hills and the mountains and the oceans...And all I seen was a bunch of niggers dazed out of their wooly heads. And Mr. Jesus Christ standing there in the middle of them grinning...He grin that big old grin...and them niggers wallowing at his feet.[35]

Martha tells him Jesus bled for him, but Loomis does not accept the doctrine. "I don't need nobody to bleed for me. I can bleed for myself."[36]

The imbalance of power bred by subservience to a white man's God is but one manifestation of the imbalance of power between black men and white man—even white men who seem interested in offering help. It is this particular relationship which interests both Wilson and Baraka. In Baraka's early plays, the white villains tend to be liberals who, according to Baraka, are dangerous in their false allegiance and professed understanding. Wilson revisits these men who claim to aid the African American, while acting mostly in their own interest.

In *Joe Turner's Come and Gone*, Selig, the "people finder" to whom Loomis has come for help in locating his wife, describes his history.

> ...we been finders in my family for a long time. Bringers and finders. My great-granddaddy used to bring nigras across the ocean on ships. That wasn't no easy job either. Sometimes the winds would blow so hard you'd think the hand of god was set against the sails...Me and my daddy have found plenty of nigras. My daddy, rest his soul, used to find runaway slaves for the

plantation bosses...Had him a reputation stretched clean across
the country.[37]

In *Ma Rainey's Black Bottom,* Ma's manager, Irvin, is described by
Wilson as a man "who prides himself on his knowledge of
African Americans and his ability to deal with them."[38] Irvin, however, cannot remember the band members' names. He tries to
sweet-talk Ma in order to make the recording go more smoothly,
but Ma recognizes his intentions.

> Irvin right there with the rest of them. He don't care nothing
> about me either. He's been my manager for six years, always
> talking about sticking together, and the only time he had me in
> his house was to sing for some of his friends.[39]

White men who offer false promise to the black man—Irvin, Selig,
the butcher in *Two Trains Running* who denies Hambone the ham
he has promised him in return for his work—all represent a
reminder by Wilson, an echo of Baraka's warning against depen-
dence on those who profess sympathy but whose actions reveal
ignorance or benign neglect, at best.

Baraka's outrage and energy inspired Wilson to expose the
exploitation of African Americans. But the nature of the battles
waged by their characters is very different. In Baraka's most violent plays, his antagonists are human. In contrast, and reflecting
the inspiration provided by the last "B," Jorge Luis Borges, Wilson
often pits his characters against antagonists who are metaphysical.
They include Mr. Death in *Fences,* the ghost of a plantation owner
in *The Piano Lesson,* and Jesus Christ in *Joe Turner.* As Wilson takes
his everyday imagery from Bearden and Baraka, he takes his mystical imagery from Borges.

Complex dramas of man's relationship to the universe,
Borges' tales are elliptical and metaphorical stories with central
characters who travel twisted paths always to a point of little hope.
It is at this juncture that some fantastic, irrational event occurs,
offering the possibility of spiritual salvation, of release from the
world of oppression and death. Several Wilson plays follow this
model, but none more clearly than *Joe Turner's Come and Gone,* in

which Wilson strove to incorporate the complexity of Borges' mystical vision into contemporary drama.

The play recalls Herald Loomis being taken prisoner by Joe Turner, who lured men into gambling, arrested them, and forced them to work his land. After seven years of servitude, Loomis begins his journey in search of his family and, ultimately, of himself. He follows one road after another, maintaining his purpose, but losing touch with his world. Finally, he arrives at the boardinghouse where he must wait for the return of Selig, the traveling salesman who claims to be able to reconnect separated families and who has agreed to help Loomis locate his wife.

As Loomis waits, he has a terrifying vision.

> I done seen bones rise up out of the water. Rise up and walk across the water. Bones walking on top of the water. Come to this place...to this water that was bigger than the whole world. And I looked out...and I seen these bones rise up out the water. Rise up and begin to walk on top of it....They just walking across the water...and then...they sunk down...when they sink down they made a big splash and this here wave come up...It washed them out of the water and upon the land. Only...only...They got flesh on them...Just like you and me![40]

In his vision, Loomis tries to walk with the bones people but cannot because he refuses to recognize his connection to them; he refuses to acknowledge that he has been deeply affected by his bondage. But Loomis' vision of the bones people, a metaphoric representation of those who died during the middle passage and early slavery and who are now rising to take their place in the world, ultimately forces him to recognize his place in the world, the place for which he has been searching. The history of Loomis' people is slavery; Loomis' history, too, is slavery. His destiny is to acknowledge his chains, then break them and take responsibility for himself. At the play's close, Loomis physically slashes his chest and metaphorically frees himself from the bondage he finally acknowledges. Far from the crippled man Loomis was when the bones people first come upon him, he ends the play "shining."

Wilson invests great power in Loomis' action.

> Loomis has been held down and he has been told that he is
> worthless. For him to understand that there's a value to his exis-
> tence, that it's an act of the creator, is a way for him to plug him-
> self into a larger universal scheme of things. This is what he
> does by accepting responsibility for his own presence in the
> world; he recognizes a greater reality.[41]

Wilson's tale is as fantastic as any told by Borges and the effect is
the same. And for his character, as for Borges' characters, it is
this extraordinary event, an unworldly vision leading to an understanding of his destiny, which releases Loomis from his mental
bondage and ends his struggle.

In much of his work, Borges portrays man as being buried by
the weight of everyday reality, blind to a larger, richer version of
possibilities, and therefore incapable of living a full and free life.
Whether Wilson was directly influenced by Borges' ideology, or
whether Borges' work resonated so deeply within Wilson because
it mirrored his own underlying philosophy, is unclear. But certainly, Wilson's central characters, Levee in *Ma Rainey's Black
Bottom*, Troy in *Fences*, Berniece in *The Piano Lesson*, Loomis in *Joe
Turner's Come and Gone*, have all closed themselves off, severely
limiting their perspectives on their lives. Their inability to
acknowledge their connection to an archetypal consciousness,
their connection to a world greater their own, an infinite world, is
ultimately self-destructive. In *The Piano Lesson*, Berniece is emo-
tionally crippled, filled with hate and rage; she cannot begin to
approach her heirloom piano, alive with the spirits of her ancestors. But at the end of the play, when her brother, Boy Willie, is
wrestling with the ghost of the landowner who enslaved their
forefathers, Berniece sits down at the piano. Wilson's stage direction explains what follows.

> She begins to play. The song is found piece by piece. It is an old
> urge to song that is both a commandment and a plea. With each
> repetition it gains in strength. It is intended as an exorcism

and a dressing for battle. A rustle of wind blowing across two continents.[42]

It is only when the characters tap into the wellspring of their history and their culture that they are empowered. Wilson believes that individual strength and transcendence is achieved through connections to a larger universe. This ideology was reinforced by the imagery of all of Wilson's primary influences.

Although Wilson's connection to Borges may seem tenuous, it is, in fact, at the very core of his work. Wilson first uncovered Borges in *The New Yorker* magazine. He then sought out more of his poetry and short stories, intrigued by his technique of foretelling the ending at the beginning.

> Borges will tell you what's going to happen. In one story, I can't remember the name of it, he wrote: "That Rodrigo would become the leader of an outlaw gang and end up with a bullet in his head would have been, at the outset, a very unlikely scenario. He was born in this town," and such and such. Then he places this guy as far away as he can from being a leader of an outlaw gang and right away, you're intrigued, because you know what is going to happen. The intrigue is how this happened. I thought that it would be a great way to write a play.[43]

Wilson tried to do so in his first draft of *Fences*, beginning with the day of Troy's funeral and moving backward to review his life. Although Wilson ultimately wrote this play in a more traditional, linear progression, he did make use of Borges' method in his most recent play, *Seven Guitars*. As the play opens, its characters are coming back from the funeral of Floyd Barton. In the next scene, a flashback, Floyd is alive. Throughout the remainder of the play, the audience witnesses the events that lead inevitably to Floyd's death. It is a compelling structure, forcing the audience to focus not on *what* happens but rather on *how* it happens. The image is established — it must then be defined.

As Wilson honed his method of creation, he experimented with forms, techniques, and themes addressed by Baraka,

Bearden, Borges, and the blues. And from these sources, he drew the images which inspire his work. Then he added to the images material from history and from contemporary life, revealing how the characters arrived at the moment in time captured by the powerful image with which he begins. Through this methodology, Wilson and his four "B's" have provided a profound decade-by-decade aural, visual, and literary portrait of African-American life in this century.

The Consequence of Tolerance

The Development of
Ma Rainey's Black Bottom

August Wilson had been listening to the blues for eleven years when he began work on *Ma Rainey's Black Bottom*. Bessie Smith had led him back to Ma Rainey, and on the day in 1976 when he decided to start a new play, Wilson was listening to one of Ma Rainey's records. He began writing, inspired by the words of the blues songs echoing off the turntable.

The original work had only five characters; it did not include the four band members who are ultimately central to the play. Wilson wrote for several months, but created only a few scenes. Then, in 1981, after listening to several recordings by male blues singers, Wilson returned to work on the play. "I suddenly realized there were these four musicians there, waiting in the band room. In them, I found the key to the play—the divisions, the tensions, the meaning of their lives."[1]

Energized anew by the music, Wilson worked quickly, trying to meet a deadline for submission to the Eugene O'Neill Theater Center's National Playwrights Conference. He wrote for two months, incorporating the scenes he had written five years earlier, which focused on *Ma Rainey*, into his new play about the band. Then he summoned up his courage to once again submit his work for consideration by the O'Neill committee. Wilson had already had two scripts rejected by the committee when he submitted *Ma Rainey's Black Bottom*. But in the spring of 1982, Wilson received a telegram. From a pool of over one thousand plays, his work had been selected for the summer writing conference. Lloyd Richards, Director of the Conference, vividly remembers his response to *Ma Rainey*:

> The talent was unmistakable. The characters were alive. They
> were people I had met in the barbershop on Saturday morning,
> talking about baseball, philosophy, politics. You'd hear humor,
> imagery, poetry — the poetry of oppressed people who have to
> create a sense of freedom in their words, people living more in
> their vision than their actuality.[2]

Ma Rainey was developed at the O'Neill Playwrights Conference in 1982. Then, in April 1984, Lloyd Richards directed a production of the play at the Yale Repertory Theatre. Six months later, *Ma Rainey's Black Bottom* opened on Broadway at the Cort Theater. The play won the New York Drama Critics Circle Award for Best American Play and was nominated for Drama Desk and Tony Awards. Critical acclaim and audience enthusiasm rewarded Wilson for the painstaking revisions he had made on his script during the course of its development.

Ma Rainey's Black Bottom examines racism and the African-American search for identity within the context of the American music world of the 1920s. The action of the play centers on a recording session by Ma Rainey and her band in a Chicago studio. The characters are revealed in a series of scenes: Ma Rainey, Ma's girl friend, Dussie Mae, and Ma's nephew Sylvester; the four band members, Cutler, Slow Drag, Toledo, and Levee, around whom the play centers; Ma's manager, Irvin, and the recording studio owner, Sturdyvant. All afternoon the characters wait to lay down the music. Ultimately, the record is cut, but the exploitative conditions in which the recording takes place lead to a violent confrontation.

When Wilson returned to *Ma Rainey's Black Bottom* in 1981, with the realization that the relationships of the band members were central to his story, he found that Levee, the newest member of the band, emerged as the play's central character. Ambitious and volatile, Levee has seen the destruction caused by racial oppression but turns a blind eye to it now, knowing that the prize he covets — the opportunity to write and record his songs with his own band — can only be awarded by the white man. Levee is writing music in a new style and he wants Sturdyvant to produce it. So, Levee plays by the white man's rules and he loses.

Ultimately, Levee realizes that he has accepted a society that refuses to recognize his worth or allow him to contribute. His existence denied, he explodes as Wilson exposes the cost of Levee's compromise. With no other outlet for his anger, Levee stabs and kills his fellow band member, Toledo, for stepping on his shoe.

With his plot laid out and his characters created, Wilson proceeded from his first draft. And in his play of the blues, Wilson echoed Baraka's dramatic warnings of the dangers of assimilation as he clarified Levee's story through five more extensively rewritten drafts of the script. To begin, Wilson revisited Ma Rainey and her place in the play, as he realized that to tell the story of Levee he needed a clearer vision of Ma. The final drama contrasts the aspirations and actions of the two. Levee believes that music can afford him the opportunity to fulfill his potential and participate in the American dream. He sees Ma Rainey's success without understanding the compromises she has made to achieve it, witnesses Ma's modest control over her own career without acknowledging the accompanying abuse and humiliation.

Thus, the play pits Levee against Ma, but it also pits Levee against the producers, and, ultimately, Levee against his fellow band members. But in the early drafts, Levee was not a moving or compelling figure; he was reckless, personally and musically, and largely responsible for his own downfall. So Wilson's job was to subtly strengthen the character so that his failure is more Aristotelian. In the rewrite, he became a grander man undone by his tragic flaw — a misunderstanding of the balance of power which makes success on his terms impossible. Through his revisions, Wilson created a character of greater dignity by showing the audience Levee's genuine musical ability, by more clearly establishing the actively destructive role Sturdyvant plays in Levee's story, and

43

by revealing the charged emotional state of an isolated man.

Wilson began with the structure, incorporating Ma Rainey more fully into the play's action, melding the two sides of his collage, in order to successfully contrast the two central characters. Title notwithstanding, in the first three drafts which followed Wilson's return to the play in 1981, Ma did not enter until the second act. In these versions, the entire first act was set in the band room and involved only the band members.

The move toward a more integrated structure had been encouraged by Lloyd Richards. Thus, while working on the play in preparation for production at the Yale Rep, Wilson rearranged a number of scenes so that Ma enters earlier. The result is action that alternates between the upstairs recording studio, where Levee wants to be, and the downstairs band room he longs to escape. In establishing the two theatrical playing areas, and the status accruing to them, Wilson strengthens the contrast between Ma, who exists primarily in the studio, and Levee, who exists primarily in the band room. Indeed, it is Levee's longing to move up to and beyond Ma, which fuels his ultimate downfall.

Levee believes he can achieve greater success than Ma because he has a vision for a different sound; he has written a new version of Ma's standard song, "Ma Rainey's Black Bottom." At the center of Levee's conflict with Ma is the interpretation of the music. Ma understands the value of the blues she sings, how they're rooted in her people, her culture, her very soul. Levee wants to update the sound to please the white producer looking for better sales.

Levee's rejection of traditional blues is a denial of a cultural connection — a denial he makes in an effort to assimilate and cash in, but a denial which is ultimately self-destructive. In order to illustrate Levee's mistake, Wilson added a passage in which Ma defines the cultural function of the blues.

> White folks don't understand about the blues. They hear it
> come out but they don't understand how it got there. They
> don't understand that's life's way of talking. You don't sing to
> feel better. You sing cause that's a way of understanding life.[3]

The meaning of the music was also revealed through added dialogue for another band member, Cutler: "You get the understanding and you done got a grip on life to where you can hold your head up and go on to see what else life got to offer."[4]

To further illustrate his point, Wilson made music a more integral part of the characters' lives. In the revisions he did for the Yale Rep, Wilson had Ma sing to herself as she waits for the recording session to begin. The music seems to cure her aching feet and ease her unrest. In the final draft of the script, Cutler, the band leader, has a new line. Each time the band begins rehearsing, Cutler leads them in: "One, two, you know what to do."[5] It becomes a ritual revealing the comforting quality of familiar music and pointing up the uncertainty generated by Levee's desire for change. This fuller appreciation of the blues by the other characters makes clearer what is being lost with Levee's desire to move away from what he terms "jug band" music.

If Levee's pursuits, a new sound and a band of his own, were completely without merit, however, there would be little dramatic tension. Thus Wilson needed to reveal that Levee's dreams, while ill-considered, are fueled by true talent, and he made a number of additions in order to acknowledge Levee's musical ability.

Wilson had the musicians show more respect for Levee's music. At one point in the play, Sturdyvant decides that the band will record Levee's version of "Black Bottom." In the early drafts, the other members of the band are contemptuous of Levee's interpretation and break off rehearsing to indulge in a petty but protracted argument about how to play the music. In the final script, the band takes Levee's version more seriously during the rehearsal.

In the successive drafts, many of the exchanges that undercut Levee's general credibility were deleted. For example, while at the O'Neill Conference, Wilson removed a line by Slow Drag indicating that Levee just wants to be troublesome. In fact, Levee wants to be successful.

Levee knows that life has dealt him a poor hand but he believes in possibility, and Wilson needed to encourage the audience to root for the young artist despite his shortsightedness. So he revealed Levee's own passion for his new music by adding a small but revealing moment to the play. Toledo and Levee are alone in the band room and Levee is working on a new song, humming and singing to himself. "Wait till Mr. Sturdyvant hear me play that! I'm talking about some real music here, Toledo! I'm talking about real music."⁶ Levee's enthusiasm is contagious.

Wilson also took time to clarify Levee's dream of forming his band and recording music. He did so through changes made in Levee's encounter with Ma's girlfriend. In early drafts, Levee merely sweet-talks Dussie Mae. "You the kind of woman make a man forget to butter his grits. You just like one of them old balky mules you like to ride out to pasture."⁷

In a revised version of the script, Levee tries to win the woman by offering plans for his band and his career. What Wilson gains from this is twofold: first, the opportunity to show Levee describing the vision he has of his musical future; second, the chance to show even more of what is at stake for Levee—musical success will provide not only artistic and financial gains, but may provide the key to companionship as well.

Levee wants to have everything Ma has, including Ma's girlfriend. But in the later versions of the play, it becomes clear—to all but the shortsighted Levee—that the relationship between the women is insignificant. What seemed a special prize for Levee is, in fact, expendable as far as Ma is concerned. In the final version, when Ma is leaving, she invites Dussie Mae to join her, but only as an afterthought.

Levee's miscalculations result from his failure to understand the deal Ma has struck with the white world, and his inability to see the place to which the music industry has relegated her. Dialogue added in later versions makes it clear how Levee views that place.

> As soon as I get my band together and make them records like
> Mr. Sturdyvant done told me I can make, I'm gonna be like Ma
> and tell the white man just what he can do....That's the way I'm
> gonna be! Make the white man respect me.⁸

But Wilson is very careful in the play to reveal how grossly inaccurate Levee's perception is. In all the drafts of the play, Ma painfully acknowledges her position while declaring her determination to fight back: "They don't care nothing about me. All they want is my voice. Well, I done learned that, and they gonna treat me like I want to be treated no matter how much it hurt them."[9] And Wilson kept refining his portrayal of Ma's conflict with Irvin and Sturdyvant to show her constant battle to be granted even the most minimal of amenities — a Coca Cola while recording, heat in the studio. Near the end of the play, Sturdyvant tries to cheat Ma's nephew Sylvester out of his pay for reciting the introduction on the recording of "Black Bottom." Irvin tells Ma that Sylvester's money is to come out of her salary. Through a progressive series of additions to the script, Wilson clarified the circumstances to reveal how limited her ability is to fight back; she does get the money for Sylvester, but only because Sturdyvant realizes that she has not yet signed the release forms for the new record.

An arrogant Levee believes in his music, but he also believes that he will be cleverer than Ma at pleasing his white bosses. He hopes to convince Sturdyvant to hire the band he has put together to record his new songs.

Through successive drafts, Wilson refined his portrait of Sturdyvant's role in Levee's downfall to further establish the destructive nature of exploitation and the cost paid for tolerating it. In the early drafts, Levee approaches Sturdyvant when the company owner first comes to the band room. Levee wants to discuss the status of the songs he has submitted. In these drafts, Levee pursues a recording opportunity without encouragement and with a hat-in-hand tone; his colleagues accuse him of "shuffling his feet" when Sturdyvant is in the room.

In all the drafts, Sturdyvant refuses at the end of the play to allow Levee to record his songs and patronizingly pays Levee five dollars for each song he has written. But Wilson decided that Sturdyvant's final action would be more obviously exploitative if throughout the play he was seen to be more actively encouraging Levee to write the songs.

In a series of additions made for the Yale Rep production, Wilson moved Sturdyvant into this stance. In a rewritten first scene, Levee is working to finish a song in response to a direct request by Sturdyvant for more music. This addition also provides the opportunity to see Levee at work on his music. Here he is at the moment of creation, glimpsing a whole world of possibility, one that supports his miscalculation about the opportunities available to him.

When Sturdyvant enters the band room, he begins the discussion by asking Levee if he has finished the song, and, in this rewritten version, Levee actually plays a section of the new song. Again, Wilson presents an energetic and hopeful Levee, and an enthusiastic and encouraging Sturdyvant. In the final version of the opening scene of the play, Sturdyvant checks eagerly with Irvin to be sure that Levee will be attending the recording session. Demonstrating the fervor of his interest increases the audience's awareness of his subsequent betrayal

In the first three drafts, in his final scene, when Sturdyvant tells Levee that he will not record his songs, Levee responds, "I wanna hold you to what you told me." [10] In the final version, this line was cut. He just keeps trying to sell his music on its merits and its potential for Sturdyvant; "That music is what people is looking for. They's tired of jug-band music." [11] Levee wants to be appreciated for his artistry. Only when Levee realizes that this approach is going nowhere does he resort to trying to win on ethical grounds:

> STURDYVANT: Well, Levee, like I say...they just aren't the kind of songs we're looking for.
> LEVEE: Now, why didn't you tell me that before when I first give them to you? You told me you was gonna let me record them... What's the difference between then and now? [12]

In the first drafts, Sturdyvant "hands Levee the money and is gone in a flash." [13] In the third draft, Wilson added the direction that Levee throws the money on the floor. In the final version, the exchange is much more physically confrontational, leading more directly to the play's closing action.

[Sturdyvant] attempts to hand Levee the money, finally shoves it in Levee's coat pocket and is gone in a flash. Levee follows him to the door and it slams in his face. He take the money from his pocket, balls it up and throws it on the floor.[14]

Levee's devastation results from the huge investment he had made in his quest for validation in the world—nothing less than his self-respect, which could not be maintained in the face of his servility. Left shattered and angry, Levee becomes violent.

In order to increase the tension which leads to the play's final moment, Wilson honed the band room scenes, tightening dialogue and increasing the pace. Specific textual changes also helped to set up the concluding dramatic action. In the Yale Rep version, Wilson added discussion of the new shoes Levee has purchased. The shoes are very important to Levee who associates them with his opportunity for success. As Levee puts them on, he lights up; "Yeah. Now I'm ready! I can play me some good music now."[15] Early in the play, this detail seems merely entertaining; but it establishes the context for the final confrontation between Levee and Toledo.

Ultimately, when Toledo steps on Levee's shoes after the scene with Sturdyvant, Levee makes an emotional leap from the damage done to them to the death of his recording career. Levee is unable to effectively challenge Sturdyvant, but he can kill Toledo.

Wilson made another small, shoe-related change as the play moved from the Yale Rep to Broadway. In the earlier draft of the play, in the first scene, Slow Drag almost steps on Levee's shoes. When Levee complains, Slow Drag responds, "Boy, ain't nobody done nothing to you."[16] Here Slow Drag's line is a denial of physical harm. In the final version, Slow Drag steps on Levee's shoes. Levee complains and Slow Drag responds, "Boy, ain't nobody done nothing to you."[17] In this last draft, it becomes a denial of emotional harm, indicating the inappropriateness of Levee's tremendous concern for the state of his shoes.

Wilson intended to present Levee as a man whose extreme overreactions are dangerous. But it was important for the themes Wilson wanted to develop that Levee's state of mind during the final action be affected only by emotional, not physical imbalance.

49

Thus, in the fourth draft, Wilson cut a reference to Levee drinking in the band room. And in the final draft, Wilson cut a reference to Levee smoking reefer with the musicians.

By way of explaining Levee's imbalance in the absence of alcohol or drugs, Wilson made several changes. In the first drafts of the script, halfway through the play Ma instructs Cutler to replace Levee. In the version performed at the Yale Rep, Ma actually fires Levee from the band, which considerably raises the stakes of Sturdyvant's affording Levee the chance to record his songs; Levee's need for that opportunity becomes even greater. When Sturdyvant refuses, Levee is left with nothing, and he is alone.

This image of Levee in isolation is furthered by Wilson through other cuts made in the script. The first act of the play ends with Levee telling the story of the rape of his mother by eight or nine white men. In the early drafts, his story was followed by Toledo finding a newspaper and Levee criticizing him for reading more "bullshit." Later Wilson cut all of this dialogue. Levee speaks to no one after his stunning story. Everyone is silent. Finally, Slow Drag plays on his bass and sings.

> If I had my way
> If I had my way
> If I had my way
> I would tear this old building down.[18]

Wilson drafted and redrafted the play, carefully balancing false opportunity against veiled oppression, examining the tragic combination of forces which drive a man toward destruction. Wilson's first version of the full-length play contained two hastily-joined sections—the drama in the band room, the domain of the African-American men, and the drama in the recording studio, the domain of the white men. In working to create a cohesive whole, Wilson wove the two parts together.

Critics maintained that the play never overcame its bifurcated focus, but audiences seem to have found the bifurcation an apt and powerful metaphor for the inequities of the segregated world Wilson was portraying. *Ma Rainey's Black Bottom* ran for 275 performances on Broadway, introducing its playwright to a welcoming world.

The Problematic Practice

August Wilson at the Eugene O'Neill Theater Center's National Playwrights Conference

In 1978, Wilson's friend Claude Purdy showed him a brochure from The Eugene O'Neill Theater Center's National Playwrights Conference, the foremost American venue for the development of new plays. Wilson tried four times to have his work selected for the very competitive O'Neill Conference. Finally, as previously noted, in the spring of 1982, *Ma Rainey's Black Bottom* was accepted for the following summer's program, opening the door for Wilson's long involvement with the O'Neill Conference. The next year, he developed *Fences* there, and the year after that, he worked on *Joe Turner's Come and Gone*. Two years later, in 1986, the Conference was host to *The Piano Lesson*, and five years later, in 1991, Wilson served as a dramaturg at the Conference, consulting on new plays by other writers. In July 1994, he returned again as a playwright with *Seven Guitars*.

The National Playwrights Conference was established in 1966. Lloyd Richards became its Artistic Director in 1968, and he is largely credited with shaping its program. In thirty years, the Conference has developed more than 475 plays by 388 playwrights, "offering them the opportunity to work on their plays in the company of other professional theater artists."[1]

51

Each year, between 1000 and 1500 submissions of new plays are reviewed by the Conference committee. Ten playwrights are selected. In late spring, a Pre-Conference is held. Here, the playwrights read their plays aloud to an assembly of the other playwrights, along with the directors and dramaturgs who will participate in the full Conference. Following each play reading, there is discussion among all in attendance. Each playwright is then assigned a director and a dramaturg, and the three meet privately to decide on the route of development each play will follow.

For Wilson, the Pre-Conference is often his first opportunity to present his play aloud to an audience. While reading certain sections, Wilson takes great pride in the work; at other points, he is hesitant. "The parts that you don't want to read are generally where the problems are."[2]

Despite the anxiety which accompanies this first step, Wilson takes full advantage of the opportunity to read his material and gauge the response of his first audience. He then seriously considers the feedback he has received, and in the month between Pre-Conference and Conference, he rewrites.

Wilson made changes in all of his plays in preparation for the full summer Conferences. Sometimes, the changes were small; e.g. the title *Mill Hand's Lunch Bucket*, taken from the inspirational Romare Bearden painting, was changed to *Joe Turner's Come and Gone.*[3] But sometimes the changes were major, involving big cuts and crucial additions or substantial reshuffling of large sections of material. In the version of *Fences* read at Pre-Conference, the primary action of the play was a flashback; but Wilson changed the play so that it moved chronologically forward. *The Piano Lesson* originally began with Boy Willie in Berniece's house; but following Pre-Conference discussion, Wilson added a new beginning which dramatized Boy Willie's entrance.

At the opening of the summer Conference, the schedule for the presentation of the plays is posted. As the date for each play's performance approaches, playwright, director, dramaturg, and actors, cast from the Conference company, meet and read through the play. Then, for four or five days, they rehearse a staged reading. The playwrights are encouraged to rewrite during the rehearsal period.

Each play is presented twice, to an audience consisting of Conference artists and staff, visiting theater professionals, and the general public who can purchase tickets. Because the presentations are intended to showcase the writing, other aspects of the production are minimal. Actors read from their scripts and wardrobe comes from their own closets. The lighting is functional and the set modular. Although there are only two days between performances, Wilson uses this time to rewrite, sometimes very substantially. Between the two performances of *Fences*, for example, he cut forty-five minutes from the play.

The day after the second performance, all Conference participants meet for a critical discussion of the play. A panel, moderated by the Artistic Director and consisting of the playwright, the director, and the dramaturg, discusses the work done on the play —the problems they encountered and the solutions they undertook. The forum is then opened to all present to comment on the play.

Although undergoing such a public critique of one's play can be daunting, Wilson finds it inspiring.

> I get to see my plays in front of an audience. I make notes, and
> I get critiques from other participants in the Conference. I
> study them very carefully and then do another draft. It was at
> the O'Neill that I actually learned to rewrite a play and that's
> part of the process that I enjoy — the rewriting and problem
> solving, what Borges calls the problematic practice of literature.[4]

The O'Neill Playwrights Conference is a mix of high fun and high stress. It is set in Waterford, Connecticut, on the Long Island Sound, where a beautiful setting and a sandy beach offer a relaxing atmosphere. The dormitory housing at a nearby college and family-style meal service rekindle memories of summer camp. But the Conference is also a pressure-cooker environment for any playwright hoping to enter the established world of professional theater. Prominent directors, dramaturgs, actors and critics from around the country are in attendance, and reports of the work presented there will make their way to many of the nation's regional theaters. Although the environment is intended to be free from commercial considerations, Broadway producers can be seen arriving for some of the performances, and it is considered an advantage to have your play scheduled for presentation on a Friday or Saturday night.

The Conference's artists are sensitive to this issue. William Partlan has been a director at the Conference for many years.

> I would say, in defense of the O'Neill approach, it is definitely not aimed at trying to create a commercial feeling. We strive very hard to help writers to achieve what they set out to achieve, as opposed to setting out, necessarily, to achieve what will get them major commercial success. And sometimes writers really want major commercial success, and then you try to help them achieve that. I would say, however, that [the Conference] doesn't avoid commercial techniques, in some ways, only because most of us who work there work in the professional theater, and, therefore, are skilled, and our instincts and our knowledge of how to work with a play tends to move it toward a structure which we know survives and does well within the existing theatrical world.[5]

Pressure at the Conference is generated not only by visitors but also from the theater professionals who are participating. Although their intentions are good, sometimes their mere presence, not to mention their participation in the development process, can be intimidating, even damaging to the playwright. Partlan shares this concern.

> There certainly are risks for various kinds of writers, and I would say that those risks have much more to do with who that writer is than they do with any intent on the part of those who are using the development process. I think it's most dangerous when a writer really doesn't know why they've written what they've written or what they want to accomplish with what they've written.
>
> But a writer may be unprepared for the kind of input that

they're going to get, and the power of that input, because most
theater professionals believe very firmly what they believe. You
have to have strong chops in place to deal with the strong egos
you come up against in a developmental process. So I think it
can be harmful to the development of certain kinds of writers
who are more vulnerable.[6]

The play development process at the O'Neill seems to best serve
playwrights who come to the Conference with a firm sense of their
own intentions. They can work effectively on their plays within the
O'Neill parameters.

Although Wilson did not have years of experience in the professional theater before first attending the O'Neill Conference, he
brought with him a security in his writing and an ability to manage
within a complex environment. The bustle of the Conference,
rewriting under pressure, and withstanding criticism from a large
circle of established theater professionals can be overwhelming.
But Wilson quickly learned to use the Conference to his advantage. Director Amy Salz, who worked with Wilson on *Joe Turner's
Come and Gone*, admires his approach.

I found him to be kind of impervious to the O'Neill process as a
whole, in terms of really having a very strong filter for the input
that he received, which I think is absolutely valuable for a playwright working in that situation. My concerns about developmental situations like that is that their impact on a playwright
can be significant if the playwright doesn't have that skill. August
had that skill, which I think came with a certain life view that he
brought with him—even more than his work as a writer.[7]

Wilson makes changes based on instinct. As Salz says, "He had to
hear it; he had to feel how the audience was sitting in their chairs
to decide if something worked."[8]

But Wilson also actively seeks the input of others. Artists who
have worked with him speak highly of his willingness to have them
participate in the process. But Partlan, who worked with Wilson
on both *Ma Rainey's Black Bottom* and *Fences*, describes how Wilson
moderates input:

55

> In working with August there was always a sort of a gentle resistance to change—without unreasonably resisting. It was always with a sense of his own desire not to shortcut himself, not to move rashly—but to listen, carefully, and to try to fathom for himself what needed to be done.[9]

And Wilson has received his fair share of severe criticism. His unusual dramaturgy, incorporating as it does extensive storytelling and non-linear narratives, continually met with resistance. After *Ma Rainey's Black Bottom* was selected for the 1983 summer Conference, the O'Neill staff had concerns about the structure of the play. Michael Feingold, who served as Wilson's dramaturg on both *Ma Rainey's Black Bottom* and *The Piano Lesson*, remembers:

> In the selection committee, everyone had been a little tense about *Ma Rainey*. It was a very odd fish to come up in there and nobody was quite sure that there was a lot happening in it. But the talk seemed interesting and this is obviously, you know, a voice, which Lloyd [Richards] always says the O'Neill is looking for.[10]

When *Ma Rainey* was performed at Pre-Conference, the extraordinary power of Wilson's play became clear. Ironically, it inspired the participants to want to change the play. In order for it to reach a wide audience, they wanted to harness its energy in a more conventional form. Feingold was concerned.

> At Pre-Conference the performance had terrific impact. And Lloyd was quite blown out about changing the play and getting the thing to work. Edith [Oliver, the play's dramaturg] wanted it to be a play in the old Broadway sense.[11]

When Bill Partlan began work on *Ma Rainey*, he focused on cutting the play, a frequent first response to Wilson's grand, early drafts. Partlan was concerned about the play's length and unconventional narrative.

> When I first met with August after Pre-Conference we talked

through the piece itself. He was very clear about his characters and the stories that they tell and I suggested that we might want to look for places to cut and he thought that that would be okay, but didn't want to make any radical moves right away. So, as we got into rehearsal on the piece, trying to look at where the conflict builds to a point, at which action can take place. And once in a while, it felt to me as though, instead of action taking place, another story would suddenly come along. So we sort of identified likely cuts in advance, but we did none of them. We rehearsed the whole play. I think it ran, the first night, a little over three and one-half hours.

We got one hour to make cuts and changes in the script between the two performances. And in that time block, I think we cut a good forty-five minutes to an hour out of the play. And the second performance ran something in the neighborhood of two and one-half hours. And it was at that performance, the second performance, actually, that Frank Rich, who was not allowed to be there as a critic, but just came out as an interested party, came to Lloyd Richards afterward—Lloyd told me—and said, in tears, to Lloyd, "I have not been so moved in the theater for twenty years."[12]

The following year, Partlan began his work on *Fences* by encouraging cutting the text.

Questions about the length of the play also surfaced during the work on *Joe Turner's Come and Gone.* Amy Salz, the play's director, remembers that the primary issue as they approached the performance was "what to cut and when to cut it." Wilson continued to be opposed to cutting his play too soon but did ultimately follow several recommendations made by his director and his dramaturg, Edith Oliver. He remembers: "It was Edith who told me to cut Bynum's story about his passionate and tragic affair. She said, 'Beautiful story but it belongs in another play, dear.'"[13]

Now and then, Wilson is disappointed to have lost a particular speech.

I miss things. I take them out because they impede the flow of

the play at the time when we just need it to get where it was
going. A character says, "I have a story to tell." And I have to say,
"That's great, man. But, I don't want to hear no story right now."[14]

Sometimes, instead of cutting a story that seemed interruptive at
its original point in the script, Wilson was able to move it to a different place entirely. This unusual process is possible because the
stories have a beginning, middle, and end in themselves and thus
they can easily be uprooted and replanted within the body of the
play, without disrupting other action. Indeed, ultimately, such
rearranging enhances the entire play.

For Wilson, the greatest benefit of an early performance of his
work is the opportunity it provides to discover the points at which
the play is confusing. He eagerly welcomes questions that serve to
identify moments when an audience perhaps cannot follow what
is happening onstage. Sometimes, even in rehearsal, such problems can surface. Michael Feingold remembers work on *The Piano
Lesson*.

> The cast had such a hard time because there's so much back
> story to the play. There's so much that happens before it, which
> is one of the extraordinary things in it, that the cast had a very
> hard time sorting out all the generations of people being talked
> about. And I took it as one of my dramaturgy functions to make
> a genealogy of the family, and I showed it to August when I was
> done and he said, "You know, you skipped a whole generation!"
> So, obviously, even I didn't follow it. So we went back and
> clarified several things.[15]

Dissatisfaction with the conclusion of *The Piano Lesson* was also
voiced following its performances at the O'Neill Conference. In
the days after the play's critique, Wilson remembers a significant
change in the ending of the play in which Boy Willie wrestles with
the ghost of the slave-trader, Sutter:

> In the original ending, I never said what happened to the piano.

To me, it wasn't important. The important thing was Boy Willie's willingness to engage the ghost in battle. Once you have that moment, then for me, the play was over. But I found out it wasn't over for the audience which kept saying, "Yeah, but who gets the piano?"

So I was working at the O'Neill, and one day, a playwright comes up to me and he says, "So what are you doing?" And I said, "I'm trying to write the end of this play." So, he says, "Leave the lights on for a minute and tell me what happens." I said, "Boy Willie comes down the steps, picks up the dolly that he has, and throws it out the door. He can't take the piano, it just saved his life; he does recognize that, you know? No way he could take the thing. So he relinquishes his hold on the piano and goes out the door." As it turned out, I was simply cutting the lights off too soon. So it was just a matter of a little rewriting and keeping the lights on for a while.[16]

Because the O'Neill participants don't always agree, changes made by Wilson satisfied some and displeased others. For example, Michael Feingold approved of Wilson's original impulse and was disappointed with the additional scene at the end of *The Piano Lesson*,

I was very unhappy when I saw the pat ending. The first ending —the one the O'Neill staged—was the right one. With Boy Willie endlessly fighting off the ghost, and his sister and the minister endlessly playing the piano, singing their hymn. There's an image there of something which does not end. And, therefore, the play cannot end.[17]

For Wilson, the environment of the Conference is inspiring. He always looks forward to time spent at the O'Neill. "I believe its process, in a way, is what my plays are about. It's people sitting around and talking; and while they're talking, something is built together out of the talk."[18]

Steeped in theater at the Conference, Wilson not only works on his current play, but also begins his next. Salz enjoyed his foresight.

> Each summer he would have a story that he would be telling over and over and over, that really became the germ of the next play. While we were working on *Joe Turner*, I remember that he kept talking about this image that he had of a piano and an older woman teaching a young girl. And the piano had deep carvings on it and all the history of the family was there. And he kept talking about this image.
>
> He does that because he really is a storyteller—he talks a lot of it out before he ever sits down to write a word.[19]

Wilson has learned much over the years. Although he had worked as a theater director, he had never studied theater formally, and he had read very little dramatic literature. Working at the O'Neill Conference has taught Wilson a great deal, particularly about traditional dramaturgy, as evidenced in the nature of changes he has made on his scripts there: extensive cutting, a more direct narrative in *Fences*, a more conclusive ending for *The Piano Lesson*. The adjustment of Wilson's artistic outlook was noted by other Conference participants; Amy Salz remarked:

> He has become a very smart man of the theater. And he really knows craft now, which he didn't when he started. He talks about drama. But when he starts to talk about it, it's really exciting, because it's really about drama, and it's dramatic. It's about what makes something dramatic and what is good story telling.[20]

Wilson himself has commented on the development of his ability to take full advantage of the critical input.

> At the beginning, I got confused. I was still relatively new to playwriting, and a lot of the stuff people were saying, I simply

didn't understand. One playwright, he said all this stuff and I didn't know what the hell he was saying. But I knew it was right. I could tell that this is entirely what this play needs. But it wasn't in a language that I could understand.[21]

But Wilson believes that his years at the O'Neill have enabled him to work closely and constructively with others.

I got better in the sense that I can understand more of what people were saying. My own response became that I understood more and I think that consequently I was able to do better work. And if I could understand the criticisms that the people were making, I could change the work. One of the things I found by the time I worked with Michael Feingold on *The Piano Lesson* was I could use the dramaturg, which I thought was cool. Steve Robman directed it and his primary interest was getting the thing on stage, up on its feet, getting the actors moved around. So, I could talk to Michael about the ideas in the play—were they reading through—and about what he was getting. Was the concept of the ghosts confusing? I understood the collaborative process better, which I think made for a better script.[22]

Michael Feingold, who worked with Wilson in 1982 and then again in 1986, also noted a change.

He became much more assured about what he was doing. He wasn't the deeply troubled soul sorting through all this stuff and what it meant. In the intervening time he had found his vocation—he had found that this was what he was great at and what he wanted to do. So there was, in a sense, much more joy in the process for him...There was also a little more practicality.[23]

Wilson's security within his own playwriting process was evidenced at the O'Neill in 1991 and 1993, when he did not submit a play of his own for development, but Lloyd Richards invited him to participate as a dramaturg. In 1993, he was assigned to work with a young writer, Kirk Aanes, who remembers the experience clearly:

> I was slightly intimidated by him at first. You know, working with
> a Pulitzer Prize-winning playwright. But he's a playwright, he
> knows how a playwright works, and he was very good about not
> imposing his own ideas on the play. Instead, he asked a lot of
> questions to find out what the play I wanted to write was; and
> then his goal was to help me find that play. He really invests him-
> self in the process. He likes working with playwrights and he has
> a lot of gratitude toward the O'Neill and, you know, is trying to
> return the favor, I guess. And he even called me, like, a couple
> months afterwards because he had an idea for my play, which
> was amazing.[24]

O'Neill participants know that Wilson has given a great deal to the
Conference, offering advice and support to its playwrights, and it
has given him a great deal in return, professionally and personally. Wilson's artistic blossoming has brought pleasure to those who
have shared his experience. Director Amy Salz is representative of
his many admirers:

> The most wonderful thing about just watching August — I mean
> just knowing him through this whole period—has been seeing
> the flowering of this man. He was so shy when he first came.
> And he found his own strength and became this extraordinary
> man. It was all underneath before but as he got more and
> more confident, he never has lost sight of who he is and what he
> believes. He's a wonderful man. And really unique.[25]

The Complexity
of Conflict

The Development of *Fences*

August Wilson began writing *Fences* in 1982, immediately following his work on *Ma Rainey's Black Bottom* at the O'Neill Playwrights Conference. Wilson's experience at the Conference had been very positive; by the time he left, *Ma Rainey* had been scheduled for production at the Yale Repertory Theatre, and there was even talk of Broadway. But Wilson feared being a one-play playwright. And so, on the bus heading home from the Conference, he wrote the first scene of *Fences*.

Fences focuses on the family of Troy Maxson. Born in poverty in the South, Troy has fought hard throughout his life. He fought to use his talent for baseball to earn a living but was rejected by the white establishment. He fought the pressures of the street but, nonetheless, landed in prison. Now, in his middle years, Troy is fighting to uphold the lessons of responsibility he has learned, and striving to balance his own needs with those of his wife, Rose, his brother, Gabe, and his sons, Cory and Lyons. But the more he struggles to stand upright, the more he stumbles, as his dreams for his family clash with their dreams and with his dreams for himself. In pursuit of a more stable life for his son, Troy denies Cory the one thing he desires most—the opportunity to play college football. And in pursuit of self-fulfillment and the drive to feel more alive, Troy has an affair, which culminates in the death of his mistress in childbirth. Trying to act responsibly under the circumstances, Troy then brings the baby home to Rose.

Wilson found a model for his central character in his stepfather, David Bedford, whose life inspired specific events in Troy's story. Following a disappointment in sports, a serious brush with crime brought Bedford lessons of responsibility and an acceptable post-prison life. Bedford had been a football star in high school and had hoped that a college football scholarship would lead to a career in medicine. No scholarship was offered. So he robbed a store to get money to go to school, killed a man, and spent twenty-three years in prison. When he came out, Bedford met Wilson's mother and began working in the city sewer department. Bedford died in 1969 when Wilson was twenty-four.

Fences is not autobiographical. But Wilson's life does provide a cultural context in which he explores themes close to his heart. "White America pays no attention to the Troy Maxsons in this world. They see niggers as lazy and shiftless. Well, Troy is a man who is trying to fulfill tremendous responsibility."

Wilson started *Fences* with the image of a man standing in his yard with a baby in his arms, an homage to Romare Bearden's *Continuities*, which features this same image. Expanding on the image in the months following the bus ride during which he wrote the first scene, Wilson created draft after draft of the play.

The elements Wilson chose to include continued to reflect his primary cultural influences; there is reference to and use of the blues, and Troy's past and present struggles against racial oppression, reminiscent of Baraka's drama, clearly mark his personality. Also, the play examines Troy through his daily rituals. This focus reflects the influence of Romare Bearden whose inclusion of the rites of everyday life is reminiscent of African performance traditions.

But *Fences* is also very much a product of Wilson's response to commercial pressures. While his previous play, *Ma Rainey's Black Bottom*, achieved great critical and box-office success, it was faulted by many critics for its non-traditional structure and its bifurcated focus. Wilson reacted to the criticism as a direct challenge and strove to write a play with a conventional narrative, one large central character, and a more universal theme.

Thus, Wilson focused his play on the balance and conflict between the characters' commitment to family and their pursuit of personal goals. At the heart of play is the juxtaposition of the decisions Troy makes regarding his family and his choice to have an affair. Although Wilson exposes the destructive nature of this choice, the clarification of his central character in successive drafts of the script enabled the audience to understand the precariousness of the balance between taking care of other people and taking care of yourself.

Wilson's efforts to define Troy's actions and attitudes began by using Lyons, the son of his first marriage, to highlight Troy's sense of familial responsibility. Lyons is trying to make a life as a musician, but he cannot meet his bills. He often arrives on Troy's payday to borrow a few dollars, and it is during the exchange surrounding this ritual (the only interaction between these characters) that Wilson contrasts the two men. We see Troy—having just arrived home from work, tired and burdened—handing over money to the free-spirited Lyons.

But Wilson realized he could also use Lyons to highlight Troy's own selfishness at the expense of his family. Thus as the drafts progressed, Wilson moved from merely contrasting Lyons and Troy to revealing certain unacknowledged similarities between the two men and the choices they face.

Wilson first tempered his original, more singly negative presentation of Lyons so that he, like Troy, is trying to be a responsible man. Early in the first draft of the play, Troy defined Lyons for us as lazy and shiftless; although Troy's opinion may not have been objective, it was the only reference for Lyons we had. Later, Wilson deleted Troy's "lazy and shiftless" remark along with an additional line about Lyons being on welfare. He also dropped Troy's comment that if Lyons doesn't know by now how to get by in life "what hope is there for [him]?"[2] Wilson also changed Lyons' age from thirty-seven to thirty-four, allowing him a little more leeway, giving him the gift of a few more years before being held fully accountable.

Lyons' choice of a career in music provided Wilson with one of several opportunities to explore the balance a man must achieve between being true to his own needs and taking care of his family. Lyons' passion for his music philosophically parallels Troy's passion for his mistress, Alberta, with each man deriving some vital spark from the pursuit of what he loves. In Wilson's initial vision, Lyons was cavalier in his decision to be a musician and his success was modest. But if the character of Troy is to be sympathetic, if the audience is to understand his decision to have an affair, then Wilson needed to give greater validity to the search for personal fulfillment. This meant also refining his portrait of Lyons' relationship with his music.

In the early stages of his work on the play, Wilson seemed to be less supportive of the choice to pursue personal destiny at the cost of family. But as the drafts of the play progressed, Wilson gave greater credence to Lyons' pursuit of his dream by making him more successful at his music. In an early version, Lyons speaks vaguely of playing somewhere; in later versions, Lyons mentions specifically that he is playing at an established club, "The Grill." In the final draft, there is an external acknowledgment of Lyons' success by way of Troy's friend Bono, who has seen in the newspaper that Lyons is playing at "The Grill," and makes the comment that you have to be good to play there. Ultimately, Lyons' pursuits will not provide a stable career, but at this point, while he is still a young man with no children of his own, his dedication to it seems to be a viable option.

Having established that Lyons' dream of a musical career was not without merit and promise did not mean that Wilson ceased to explore the problematic ramifications of such pursuit. Music does not support Lyons. In all versions of the script, he comes to his father to borrow money on Troy's payday. In the first draft of the play, Lyons returns on the second payday to borrow again. But Wilson wanted to show that Lyons, like Troy, tries to balance conflicting responsibilities. In later drafts, Lyons returns on the second Friday to return the money he previously borrowed. Although he will borrow the same money again in the future, the return is a very important gesture and a significant change in the character; Lyons does not take the money lightly; he has every intention of repaying it.

Wilson continued to parallel Lyons and Troy through the relationship of Lyons with his wife, Bonnie (whom we never see). In the first draft, when Rose invites Lyons to stay for dinner and he responds that he has to get home to Bonnie, Troy comments: "Listen to that nigger. He got ten dollars in his pocket...time Bonnie see him it be two o'clock in the morning. Talking about he got to get home."[3] Troy makes this comment from his front porch, alongside his wife, the picture of the family man—before we learn of his affair.

But Wilson did not want Troy to appear hypocritical by consistently criticizing behavior of which he himself would later be shown to be guilty. So, in the next draft, Wilson dropped the reference to Bonnie; Lyons cannot stay for dinner because he must pick up "his horn" and get down to the club. But this version did not illuminate Lyons' tendency to abdicate family responsibility. Thus, in the final version, Rose tells Lyons that Bonnie called to say he should pick her up. Later, lacking confidence that Lyons will remember, perhaps because of her own experience with a husband's late-night returns home, she reminds Lyons of his duty.

Bearden's image of the man with the baby centers the play, and exploration of this relationship as it develops—particularly the influence of a father on a child despite the child's attempts to deny this influence—is crucial to Wilson's drama. Lyons' effort to separate himself from Troy becomes clearer as the play progresses. In the first versions, Troy criticizes Lyons' choice not to work, and Lyons responds that music helps him to get up in the morning and find his place in the world. But the response was too general to demonstrate Lyons' very explicit desire to be different from his father. In the Yale Rep version, the argument becomes more pointed as Lyons denies the validity of his father's life choices:

TROY: Why ain't you working?
LYONS: Aw Pop, You know I can't find no decent job. . .
TROY: . . .Get you on the rubbish if you want to work. . .
LYONS: Naw, Pop. . .thanks. That ain't for me. I don't wanna be carrying nobody's rubbish. I don't wanna be punching nobody's time clock.
TROY: What's the matter – you too good to carry rubbish? You too lazy to work and you wanna know why you ain't got what I got.[4]

With both his sons, Troy tries to promote responsibility to family over dedication to personal pursuits. And when faced with the young men's instincts to make the opposite choice, Troy denies that it may have been his example which guided them. He tells Rose that she's been "mothering" Cory too much, and he tells Lyons that he was "raised wrong." Troy consistently abdicates any responsibility for his sons' behavior. But it becomes clear through Troy's actions that his sons are, in fact, following in his footsteps.

Nonetheless, Lyons and Troy both believe through most of the play that they are completely different from each other, even as the audience is let in on the similarities between them. As young men, both pursued what they believed to be their personal destiny at great cost to themselves and those around them; Lyons' inability to make a life in music and Troy's inability to make a life in baseball led, for both, to loss of a first marriage and then to prison (events which occur before the play begins). Later in life, they both settle down in an effort to make peace with their circumstances. But both find a conventional, stable existence life-sapping. Thus, both contrive to stoke their life force—via music for Lyons and sexual rejuvenation for Troy. Troy tells his wife:

> I saw that girl...she firmed up my backbone. And I got to thinking that if I tried...I just might be able to steal second. Do you understand after eighteen years [of marriage] I wanted to steal second.[5]

Troy's relationship with his second son, Cory, is a vital part of the play as Wilson examines Troy's attempt to guide the boy into a responsible life. A high school senior, Cory has been recruited to play college football. But Troy will not sign the papers to permit this.

Although Wilson presents Cory's position sympathetically, he supports Troy's decision. "Blacks who received sports scholarships to go to school were exploited. Very few got an education. Troy makes the right choice when he tells his son that football won't lead anywhere. He's telling his son to get a job so he won't have to carry garbage."[6]

Despite Wilson's implicit endorsement of Troy's decision, he fully understands its negative impact on his son. And as Wilson worked on *Fences*, he continually labored over his portrayal of their relationship. In the first version of the play, there is an extended scene between Cory and Troy in which they discuss the purchase of a new television set. Cory doesn't understand why they cannot buy a TV, and Troy tries to explain the financial management of a household. The scene concludes with Troy offering to pay half if Cory can come up with the other half. Here we have an opportunity to see father and son interact in a non-confrontational manner, and also to see Troy exercising a fatherly concern for his son beyond feeding and clothing him. During work at the O'Neill Conference, this section was effectively moved from the second to the first half of the play where it serves as groundwork to inform the later conflicts between Troy and Cory.

At the Yale Rep, however, the entire section was dropped in an effort to shorten the work. But the omission of the exchange between Troy and Cory left too large a gap in the portrayal of Troy's exercise of familial responsibility. At the conclusion of the play, in all the drafts, Cory complains of a lack of understanding and emotional support from Troy, and he provokes Troy by asking him what he ever gave to his son. Troy responds: "Them feet and bones. That pumping heart. I give you more than anybody else is ever gonna give you."[7]

Troy is angry with Cory's implication that he has somehow failed the boy, for he believes that he has fulfilled his obligation to his son. With the long scene about the television having been cut, however, we can see only that Troy has provided Cory the bare bones. But Wilson wanted the audience to know that Troy has, in fact, provided more—more guidance, more support, more sympathy—and he restored the television scene in the final version.

While doing so, Wilson also gave Troy the opportunity to explain more fully his attitude toward Cory's college recruitment. In earlier drafts, Troy had challenged Cory, in anger, to give up football: "You go on and get your book learning where you can learn to do something besides carry people's garbage."[8] In Wilson's final revision, Troy is more patient, more loving and concerned, and his speech has a more inspirational quality. Wilson moved Troy from an expression of bitterness over his own life to an expression of a positive dream for his son.

> You go on and get your book learning so you can work yourself up in that A&P or learn how to fix cars or build houses or something, get you a trade. That way you have something can't nobody take away from you. You go on and learn how to put your hands to some good use. Besides hauling people's garbage.[9]

It is important to see that Troy has good intentions even as the play reveals his failings. As a younger man, Troy pursued his personal destiny in baseball at the cost of his family. Now, later in life, he professes to have made responsibility to others his priority. But Troy's efforts are neither wholehearted nor entirely successful, and Wilson uses Cory to make this point. As he revised the play, Wilson gave Cory a more mature understanding of the workings and failings of his family, particularly his father.

In early drafts, Cory was angry at his father and revealed his emotions in naive, sophomoric outbursts: "I hate your blood in me."[10] As the drafts progressed, Cory challenges Troy on substantive issues. At the play's close, in the final draft, Cory upbraids Troy for his mistreatment of Rose, "I don't know how [Rose] stand you...after what you did to her."[11] Although Cory's understanding of the issue is not complete, it goes straight to the core of Troy's view of himself as a responsible man, forcing him to come to terms with the fact that he put himself, his own fulfillment, before his responsibility to his wife.

The structure of the play leads to a dramatic confrontation, both physical and emotional, between Troy and Cory. Recognizing the flaws in his father and needing to make his own choices, Cory has become a man. There isn't room in the house for two men, and a simple argument about Troy moving over on the steps so that Cory can pass into the house blows up into the final exchange between them.

In early drafts, this final scene was potentially more violent. In the first versions, at the height of the confrontation, when Cory picks up Troy's baseball bat, Troy brings out a gun, points it at his son, and the stage directions read that he cocks the trigger.

Wilson dropped this detail before the Yale Rep production when he read that Marvin Gaye had been shot by his father. In the later drafts, the only weapon in the scene is the baseball bat, symbolically more powerful in its meaning to Troy, and dramatically more powerful, too, since it can be used as a weapon only when two people are in close physical proximity to each other.

The conflict between father and son continued to change in other ways, too. In the production at the Yale Rep, Cory swings the bat once and then retreats into the alley as Troy continues to approach. The conflict is interrupted by the arrival of Rose, prompting Cory to leave the yard.

Wilson realized that the interruption left the conflict unresolved. Thus, in the final version, Rose does not enter, and the climax of the play is more meaningful as the complex relationship between father and son is more intricately explored. Cory swings the bat once and misses. Then he swings again and misses. Troy offers him the chance to swing a third time, having positioned himself as a target impossible to miss. Now, Cory cannot swing. The two men struggle for the bat, and Troy takes it away. Troy prepares to swing, but he stops himself. Defeated, Cory leaves the yard and does not return until after Troy's death, years later. In this final version the anger between Cory and Troy is the most visceral. And yet it is in this version where we clearly see that neither one can intentionally injure the other.

Whether Cory becomes like his father or learns to be different is explored by Wilson in the final "interaction" between the two. The play concludes after a passage of eight years and the death of Troy. The issue of Cory's sense of responsibility is explored one last time through his indecision about whether to attend Troy's funeral. Wilson, like his character, changed his mind many times about whether Cory would go.

In the first draft, Cory does not attend his father's funeral. He expresses his continued bitterness to Lyons in an extensive exchange. Then, as a casualty of Wilson's feeling that the exchange between the half-brothers did not ring true, as well as his concern for the running time of the show, this long discussion was cut before the first performance at the O'Neill Conference. Cory merely wanders away during a discussion

71

between Lyons and Rose and does not return. Dissatisfied with Cory's disrespectful choice, the audience responded negatively. For the second O'Neill performance, Cory's discussion with Lyons and his subsequent departure were dropped, leaving the implication that Cory does attend the funeral.

Both of these versions were unsatisfactory to Wilson. So, in the Yale Rep version, Cory tells Rose that he is not going to the funeral and Rose, playing the role Wilson had previously assigned to Lyons, urges Cory to attend. Wilson also rearranged the scene so that the entire family surrounds the young man at the moment of his decision. Cory knows he must go to the funeral, and in this final draft, Wilson provides Cory a subtle acknowledgment of his choice as he says to his half-sister Raynell, "You go on in the house and change them shoes like Mama told you so we can go to Papa's funeral."[12]

Rose, having survived the most damaging kind of betrayal from Troy, is a powerful spokesperson for remaining true to one's commitments even without the expectation of reciprocity. In progressive drafts, Wilson carefully refined her character so that as she moved toward greater forgiveness and understanding, Troy's betrayal appeared all the more dramatic.

The most significant change in Rose was in her day-to-day relationship with Troy and how this, in turn, affects his relationship with Alberta. In the early version of the play, Rose is much more a nagging wife. She bothers Troy constantly about his drinking (which is considerably greater in the early drafts). She reprimands Troy for his neglect of Cory, and when she is tired of Troy's shouting, she tells him to go shout somewhere else. Although certainly none of these faults warrants Troy's infidelity, they perhaps provide him an excuse. As the versions progress, this side of Rose almost completely disappears, and Troy's affair seems less excusable, more stark a violation of his marital responsibility.

But Rose is tolerant—more and more so as the drafts of the play progressed. In the early versions of the play, Troy's announcement that he will be a father comes as a complete surprise to Rose. In later versions of the play, Rose suspects that he is having an affair as she catches inconsistencies in his explanations of his

72

August Wilson at the O'Neill Playwrights Conference, 1984.
Photograph by A. Vincent Scarano.

Top: Romare Bearden. *Mill Hand's Lunch Bucket.* 1978.
Collage on board.
Private Collection. Photograph by Richard Herrington.

Bottom: August Wilson watches the rehearsal of *Jitney* at the
Crossroads Theatre, 1997. Photograph by Glen Frieson.

Romare Bearden. *The Piano Lesson*. 1984. Silkscreen.
Private Collection. Photograph by Richard Herrington.

Romare Bearden.
Continuities. 1969.
Collage on board.
University Art Museum,
Berkeley, California; gift of
the Childe Hassam Fund of
the American Academy of
Arts & Letters.

James Earl Jones in the
Broadway production of
Fences, 1987. Photograph by
Ron Scherl/ StageImage.

Top: August Wilson in rehearsal for *Ma Rainey's Black Bottom* at the O'Neill Playwrights Conference, 1984. Photograph by A. Vincent Scarano.

Bottom, left to right: Steven R. Blye, Charles S. Dutton, and Robert Judd in the Yale Repertory Theatre's production of *Ma Rainey's Black Bottom*, 1984. Photograph by George Slade, courtesy of the Yale Repertory Theatre.

Top, left to right: August Wilson, William Partlan, Mary Alice, and Harold Rollins Jr. in rehearsal for *Fences* at the O'Neill Playwrights Conference, 1983. Photograph by A. Vincent Scarano.

Bottom, left to right: James Earl Jones and Courtney B. Vance in the Broadway production of *Fences*, 1987. Photograph by Ron Scherl / StageImage.

Top, left to right: August Wilson and Lloyd Richards confer at the O'Neill Playwrights Conference, 1984. Photograph by A. Vincent Scarano.

Bottom, foreground, left to right: Charles S. Dutton and Ed Hall in the Seattle Repertory Theatre's production of *Joe Turner's Come and Gone*, 1987. Photograph by Chris Bennion.

Top, left to right: August Wilson and Walter Dallas in rehearsal for *Jitney* at the Crossroads Theatre, 1997. Photograph by Glen Frieson.

Bottom, foreground, from left to right: Curtis McClarin, Jerome Preston Bates, Stephen M. Henderson, and Peggy R. Johnson in the Crossroads Theatre's production of *Jitney*, 1997. Photograph by Glen Frieson.

whereabouts, but she says nothing.

When Troy finally tells his wife about Alberta, Rose preaches the bible of familial responsibility.

> I gave eighteen years of my life to stand in the same spot with you. Don't you think I ever wanted things? Don't you think I had dreams and hopes?...Don't you think it ever crossed my mind to want to know other men? That I wanted to lay up somewhere and forget about my responsibilities?...But I held on to you, Troy...I took all my feelings, my wants and needs, my dreams...and I buried them inside you...I held on to you, Troy.[13]

In the second, third, and fourth drafts of the script, there is no further mention of the affair until Troy brings home the baby. But in the final version, Wilson chose to extend the duration of Rose's tolerance by reinserting an original scene which had been cut to shorten the script. Here, six months after Rose learns of Troy's infidelity, she confronts him about his continuing attention to Alberta, telling him he's living on "borrowed time" with her.[14] Rose retains her composure and her emotional charge as she points out the fallacy in Troy's theory that his physical presence in bed at the end of every night fulfills his obligation to his household regardless of where he has been up to that time.

As Rose grows more philosophical, even under the burden of a betrayal that she understands to be ongoing, our sympathy for her becomes stronger. And Rose's eventual decision to accept Troy's bastard child but to sexually renounce its father—the same in all drafts of the play—makes more sense as the action of a woman who, over time, has come to recognize the impossibility of change in her husband.

Rose stands in the center of the play as a model of responsibility but also as an example of the cost of responsibility to others at the expense of self. In response to Troy's explanation of his affair, Rose responds that she also has needs and wants not satisfied at home. But ultimately she sees no options for herself simply because, as she explains to Troy, "You my husband."[15]

Rose's selflessness moves toward an ultimate commitment

outside of herself—that is, to the church. In successive versions of the play, Rose becomes more involved with the church, participates more in its events, sings more of its hymns, and ends the final version of the play completely engrossed in the institution.

Troy remains independent, somehow able to reconcile to his own satisfaction a complex range of conflicting needs and desires. Wilson performed a complicated balancing act of his own to get the audience to be sympathetic to the choices Troy makes, even to support them. He accomplished this through careful selection of the details, choosing those that would highlight Troy's concern with personal autonomy, dignity, self-realization.

Interestingly, as the character progressed, Troy shifted from the Baraka-influenced character, who was more clearly politically controlled and motivated, to a more individualistic and ultimately more universal character. In the early drafts, Troy was an active crusader for social justice. But as the play progressed, his compassionate references to those on the street, those who had been dealt a bad lot, along with his comments on how African Americans should treat other African Americans, all disappeared. The result is that his remaining concerns regarding equality are more personally focused—on his right to drive the garbage truck previously driven only by whites, or his desire to have Rose shop at the more expensive Bella's market where Troy has been extended credit.

Wilson wanted to portray Troy as a man who consciously and freely chooses the road he will follow—for better or for worse. He supported this with numerous script changes relating to Troy's behavior and beliefs. For example, his liquor consumption is greatly reduced with each draft. In an early version, Troy refers to drinking as a way "to get a break from being responsible," and so it was a natural choice for Wilson to change this detail and deny Troy this crutch.[16]

Over time, Wilson also reevaluated Troy's religious commitment. In the first draft, following Alberta's death in childbirth, Troy rails at Jesus, asking for salvation in the face of his trials. This speech, combined with other religious rhetoric, presents a Troy who feels that God is ultimately in control of his destiny. But Wilson didn't want to offer Troy any chance to abdicate responsibility, and so he moved him away from an inherently religious position.

At the O'Neill Conference, the salvation speech and similar references to God were dropped. Through the next few drafts, Wilson provided Troy with numerous mentions of the devil and his general tone, though humorous, is much more sacrilegious. During development at the Yale Rep, Wilson added a speech for Troy following Alberta's death. Troy challenges "Mr. Death" to try to come for someone close to him or Troy himself: "You come up and knock on the front door. Anytime you want. I'll be ready for you."[17] Thus, Troy's sense of being responsible for his own fate has changed markedly.

Troy makes his decisions with a fully-developed sense of self-determination but, as the drafts progress, he makes them with ever-less feeling for their consequences. In an early draft, Troy comments on Cory's disobedience: "You wanna be grown...wanna do what you wanna do...alright. But when the time comes to pay the consequences...you got to pay them...that go for me too."[18] Although this statement would prove prophetic for Troy regarding his own actions, he does not at the time recognize it as applying to himself, and so the line was cut.

Changes in the way Troy justifies his affair to his friend Bono also reflect Wilson's sense of him as a man who is, most of all, true to himself. In all the drafts, Bono reminds Troy of Rose's goodness and tells Troy, "You responsible for what you do." In the early drafts, Troy says he accepts responsibility for his action, that he has thought about what he's doing. In later drafts, this part of the speech is cut, and the remainder reads differently: "I ain't ducking the responsibility of it. As long as it sets right in my heart...then I'm okay. Cause that's all I listen to. It'll tell me right from wrong every time." Driven more heavily by his emotions, Troy has not fully considered the harm his actions can do to others. Despite what Troy preaches to all the other characters in the play, ultimately he puts responsibility to himself above his responsibility to them.

Indeed, none of the characters finds a successful balance. Lyons, following his father's example, pursues some badly-needed cash straight into jail. Rose, fearing her husband's example, denies her own dreams in a selfless devotion to her church. And Cory, having had his dream denied him, joins the army. For Wilson, society's institutions loom as forces which often engulf and guide the lives of those who cannot create within themselves the delicate balance between need and obligation, desire and responsibility, self and others.

The four available drafts of *Fences* reveal the changes which survived pads and paper napkins and five years of evolution. Written in 1982, *Fences* was developed at the O'Neill Theater Playwrights Conference in July 1983. In April 1985, *Fences* opened at the Yale Repertory Theatre, and, later that year, it moved to the Goodman Theatre. *Fences* then played in Seattle and in San Francisco, and it opened on Broadway in March 1987.

Working on his play around the country afforded Wilson the opportunity to listen to the opinions of many theater artists and laymen about his work. Some ideas were incorporated and some rejected. At the encouragement of another playwright, Wilson made Troy's relationship with Alberta more overt. Yet Wilson rejected a producer's idea to have Troy's brother, who believes himself to be the Saint Gabriel blowing the horn to open the gates of heaven, play the saxophone as opposed to the trumpet.

Wilson cut a mass of material from the play in an attempt to accommodate contemporary time expectations. *Fences* ran three and one-half hours during its second performance at the O'Neill Conference. The play was cut significantly before rehearsals at the Yale Rep, but another 30 minutes had to go prior to Broadway, thereby bringing the play to its two and one-quarter hour playing time.

From the play's inception and continuing through its development, Wilson pursued his goal to make *Fences* a more traditional play than those he had previously written, and he succeeded. Of all Wilson's plays, *Fences* most closely follows orthodox western views of tragic form, and it was his greatest commercial success. Runs at regional theaters throughout the country sold out, and the Broadway production grossed eleven million dollars in one year.

Because of its conventional structure and the streamlined nature of its character development, *Fences* is prime material for the study of the development of a playwright's vision for a single play. The play has a simplicity in the direct relationship between Troy and each of the other characters and in the direct impact of each of these relationships on the presentation of the play's main themes.

The audience's ability to understand the complexity of the conflicts within the characters is central to the effectiveness of the play. Many of the characters in *Fences*, like those in our lives, make what seem to be irresponsible choices. Wilson's aim was to examine such choices by revealing the pressures that influence each of them, and ultimately to uncover the nobility and dignity of every individual.

The Cultural
Connection

The Development of
Joe Turner's Come and Gone

August Wilson was thumbing through a *National Geographic* magazine when he came upon a painting by Romare Bearden entitled
Mill Hand's Lunch Bucket. The image of the man at the center of
the painting, a dark and haunting figure, seemed to speak to
Wilson, asking for his story to be told.

> *Mill Hand* was a painting of a boardinghouse scene with four
> figures: an abject man with a coat and a hat sitting at a table,
> another man reaching for his lunch bucket, and a woman who
> was leaving the house, and a child with a glass of milk. I began
> to wonder who was this defeated man sitting at the table?[1]

At the time Wilson discovered the painting, he was writing a poem
about a newly-freed slave trying to reunite with his family. By combining the story line of his poem with the image of the mysterious
figure in Bearden's painting, Wilson created Herald Loomis, and
began a play in which he was the central character. And he found
Loomis' history in an old blues song, "Joe Turner's Come and
Gone," which bemoaned the fate of young African-American men
who were captured at the turn of the century by Joe Turney,
brother of the governor of Tennessee.[2] Turney lured the men

into gambling, which was illegal, and then, as punishment, had them serve a term of peonage on his plantation. In Wilson's play, Herald Loomis became a man who was separated from his wife when he was forced into servitude to the infamous "Joe Turner."

Wilson originally titled his play *Mill Hand's Lunch Bucket*, after the painting. But he set his play in 1911, a decade before the time the painting depicts, in order to incorporate the real-life figure of Joe Turner, and to be closer in time to the Emancipation. As Wilson envisioned the events of his character's life, he saw the seven years of Loomis' bondage as metaphorically representative of all the years of African-American slavery, and Loomis' search for identity as emblematic of the need of the newly-freed slaves to reconnect with their families and themselves.

At the beginning of the play, Loomis arrives in Pittsburgh with his daughter, Zonia. For three years, they have been searching for Loomis' wife, Zonia's mother. Loomis finds a room at the boardinghouse of Seth and Bertha. There, he meets Selig, a white man called the "People Finder," whose travels as a salesman sometimes enable him to reunite separated families. Loomis pays Selig a dollar to find his wife.

During the course of the play, as Loomis waits for Selig's return, Wilson introduces the boardinghouse owners, Seth and Bertha, along with their boarders: Bynum, a conjurer; Jeremy, a young man who has come to seek his fortune up North; Mattie, a young woman recently abandoned by her man; and Molly, a traveler and modern woman. Through his encounters with these characters, Loomis rediscovers his identity, freeing himself from the emotional bondage which lingers long after physical enslavement has ended.

Joe Turner's Come and Gone (the title was changed in the third draft) was presented first as a reading at New Dramatists Play Center in New York City. Then, following a familiar path, Wilson developed it at the Eugene O'Neill Theater Center's National Playwrights Conference, and premiered it at the Yale Repertory Theatre in 1986. After its run in New Haven, *Joe Turner* was presented at the Huntington Theater Company in Boston, the Seattle Repertory Theater, the Arena Stage in Washington, D.C., and the

Old Globe in San Diego. The play opened on Broadway at the Ethel Barrymore Theater on March 18, 1988.

During this five-year period of development and production, Wilson repeated the process he had undertaken with previous plays, continually modifying the script to clarify his characters and consequently, his themes. Wilson revisited the issue of responsibility, so central to *Fences*. But in *Joe Turner*, taking responsibility for oneself involves defining one's personal and cultural identity. The refining of the play centered on illuminating the search of each character for his or her place in the world—a search which can only reach successful conclusion when the past is carried forward into the present and the future.

Joe Turner is a call to reestablish cultural connections; i.e. to recognize the link between personal and cultural history, and to incorporate the older African traditions into contemporary lives. Thus, as *Joe Turner* was revised, Wilson focused on enriching the character of Bynum, the conjurer. Through Bynum, he hoped to show the continuing role of African mysticism in the lives of his characters and the potential of what Wilson terms "African retentions," which, in his view, can serve as both a source of strength and a kind of psychic balm for twentieth-century African Americans. It was the interactions between Bynum and Loomis that enabled Wilson to illustrate this theme most powerfully.

To achieve maximum dramatic impact, Wilson had to alter the characterization of Bynum in various ways, increasing his spirituality and intensifying the power of his faith, so that the audience could understand his impact on Loomis. Bynum is the most mystical character in *Joe Turner*, a man dedicated to finding what he calls another "Shiney Man." The first Shiney Man was someone he met on the road many years before who seemed to emanate light. The Shiney Man gave Bynum the secret of his life—showed him the path he was to follow on a journey that would not be complete until he disovered another Shiney Man. Bynum's encounter with his Shiney Man gave him his connection to a larger continuum in which he found his song, the play's metaphor for self-definition and life's purpose. Bynum chose the Binding Song:

"Been binding people together ever since. That's why they call me Bynum. Just like glue I sticks people together."[3] Discovery of another Shiney Man will indicate to Bynum that he has completed his life's work. Having built his future from the stones of his past, Bynum will have left his mark on society—and he will have fulfilled his destiny.

In addition to making his own search, Bynum is a spiritual agent for all the other characters, a catalyst for their searches. Thus, for the play to work, the audience must accept Bynum as an authentic conjurer, and it became Wilson's task to isolate Bynum from the more commonplace elements of life and to evince his potential power.

Initially, in earlier drafts, Wilson cut references to Bynum as a physical being; e.g. discussion of his age or his tendency to overeat, details that undercut his spirituality. Also, early on in his revisions, Wilson eliminated a story Bynum told of lost love, passion, and suicide, leaving him, instead, with women who exist only in "memory time."[4]

Wilson created distance between Bynum and the other characters by making him more even-tempered in contrast to their volatility. In early drafts, Bynum is easily offended and a bit hot-tempered. In later versions, he no longer argues with the other characters, but lets their critical comments roll off his back. Beyond the pettiness of daily life, he focuses his energy elsewhere.

Bynum is differentiated from the other characters, but he is still very much a part of the world. Just as they go off to work every morning, so does Bynum, only *his* work is the exercise of his mystical energy. As the drafts progressed, Wilson added dialogue which helped portray Bynum going about the practice of his art. Before bringing *Joe Turner* to the O'Neill Conference, Wilson revised the play so that it began with Seth watching Bynum through the kitchen window and describing the actions he undertakes each morning; Bynum draws a circle in the dirt, digs a small hole, kills a pigeon, and drips its blood on the ground.

In the version rewritten for the Yale Rep, Wilson gave Bertha a new speech later in the play which again describes Bynum practicing his magic.

> He been out there in that yard all morning. He was out there
> before the sun come up. He didn't even come in for breakfast.
> I don't know what he's doing. He had three of them pigeons
> lined up out there. He danced around till he get tired. He sit
> down awhile then get up and dance some more. He come
> through here a little while ago looking like he was mad at the
> world.[5]

It is an important addition, reminding the audience of Bynum's
constant conjuring. The repetition lends credence to the role
Bynum's magic plays in the reunion of Loomis and his wife,
Martha, at the play's conclusion.

Wilson also made additions that convey the fact that for
Bynum magic is a business. Early in the play, Mattie comes to the
boardinghouse to seek the assistance of Bynum in reconnecting
with her lover. In the Yale Rep version, Wilson added lines in
which Mattie asks about paying Bynum, and he accepts the two
quarters she offers. Although this interaction might seem to
tether Bynum too much to everyday reality, in fact it makes his
conjuring more believable because the audience sees that he
actually makes his living by it.

On the other hand, Wilson chose to eliminate another mon-
etary reference. While working on the play at the O'Neill
Conference, Wilson had given Molly a line suggesting that if
Bynum could bottle his magic, he'd get rich. Because he felt, in
retrospect, that the line brought to mind a charlatan, Wilson cut
it during the second O'Neill performance.

To better define Bynum's character, Wilson made a point of
juxtaposing Bynum and Selig. Bynum is, as he says, a Binder. He
has the power to bring people together—a power derived from
faith and strength of spirit. The other character in the script who
brings people together is, of course, Selig, the People Finder, who
accidentally discovers people's lost relatives while selling pots
and pans. Selig will be the one to physically find Loomis' wife,
Martha, and bring her back to the house. But Wilson's portrayal

of Selig, continually emphasizing his limited understanding in contrast to Bynum's tremendous insight, validates the role of Bynum's magic in the reunion at the end of the play. When the simple Selig arrives with Martha, it is clear that his actions have been guided by a greater force.

Both men's skill at bringing people together has been passed on through generations, and both men retain something of the character of their forebears. Bynum's father, himself a healer, helped Bynum find his Binding Song. Selig's grandfather was a "bringer," working on the ships which transported Africans into slavery. From his blood, his past, Bynum drew enlightenment, while Selig has inherited a kind of blindness. In a line added for the O'Neill Conference, Selig describes the difficulties of his grandfather's job. He says without irony, "Sometimes the winds would blow so hard you'd think that the hand of God was set against the sails."[6]

But Wilson wanted Selig to remain sympathetic. Thus, during his work for the Yale Rep, he eliminated Selig's description of his father's ability to find missing slaves: he could "smell a runaway nigger for miles." He also replaced Selig's use of "nigger" with "nigra."[7]

By contrasting Selig's perspective with that of Bynum, Wilson highlighted the depths of Bynum's humanity. In all the drafts, Bynum delivers a beautiful homage to women in the hope of encouraging Jeremy to offer them greater respect. "A woman is everything a man need. To a smart man she water and berries. And that's all a man need. That's all he need to live on."[8] In the second draft, Selig is given a new speech describing his relationship with his horse, who has become his principal companion since his wife locked him out of his house.

Bynum knows Selig has no power beyond that of running into people others are seeking, but he continues to challenge Selig to find his Shiney Man, thus encouraging Selig's spiritual awareness. Bynum tells Selig of his encounter with the Shiney Man and his discovery of the secret of existence. When Selig complains that he cannot find any secrets in Bynum's ramblings, Bynum responds, "Can't nobody figure it out for you. You got to come to it on your own."[9]

At the end of the play, Bynum's Shiney Man is revealed to be Herald Loomis. Over successive drafts, Wilson made a number of key changes in Bynum's description of the Shiney Man to support this conclusion. One involved the timing of his description, which was moved from the third scene to the first scene of the play, before the arrival of Herald Loomis, thus laying a foundation for the encounter. Wilson also included new details in Bynum's Shiney Man speech which would enable the audience to accept Loomis as a Shiney Man. Bynum first undercuts the idea that a Shiney Man is immediately recognizable. "He's just a man I seen out on the road. He ain't had no special look." [10] Then Bynum includes the detail that "there was lots of Shiney Men." [11]

Wilson further sets up Loomis as a Shiney Man with the addition of the detail that the first Shiney Man had told Bynum to rub blood over his body as a way of cleansing himself. Loomis will perform this act at the end of the play as Bynum proclaims him to be "shining like new money." [12] It is an extremely rewarding moment: Bynum is fulfilled, having rediscovered, or perhaps recreated a Shiney Man; Loomis is truly free; and the audience has been a witness to the full arc of the experience resulting in this transcendence. Interestingly, Wilson changed a stage direction so that Loomis has moved offstage before Bynum sees him shine. This enabled the audience to accept Bynum's vision without the aid of stage effects.

In the Yale Rep script, Wilson also added a definition of the Shiney Man as the "One Who Goes Before and Shows the Way." [13] When applied retrospectively to Loomis at the play's conclusion, this definition adds great resonance to Loomis' efforts to find his place in the world, suggesting that they represent an effort which all must undertake.

Bynum's involvement with Loomis' search is central to the play and to understanding both characters. Having created Bynum's history and established him as a practitioner of mystic arts, Wilson made significant changes to clarify Bynum's role in the reunion Loomis has with his wife and the spiritual awakening he has within himself.

It was important to show that Bynum did not physically bring about the reunion. So, step by step, Wilson distanced

Bynum from the literal logistics of Loomis' search. In the first draft of the script, Bynum mentions to Selig that Loomis is looking for someone, and it is as a result of this exchange that Loomis sends Selig to search for his wife. In the second draft of the script, Bynum actively encourages Loomis to seek out Selig to work on his behalf, telling him "You got to see Rutherford Selig if you wanna find somebody. Selig's the People finder." [14] But during the work he did in preparation for production at the Yale Rep, Wilson cut these references. Instead, Loomis seeks out and employs Selig on his own, and it seems that Bynum's mere presence facilitates Loomis' first step toward establishing independence.

This change also afforded Wilson the opportunity to continue to move Loomis down the road to discovery. By the end of the play, Loomis realizes that Bynum has somehow participated in his journey. But since Bynum had no tangible involvement in the search for Martha, Loomis must look below the surface to see the connection, to acknowledge that Bynum's mysticism was the magic that brought Loomis and his wife together—not so they can reunite, for neither wishes to do so, but so that Loomis can end his search and Zonia can be with her mother again. By recognizing Bynum's power, Loomis takes a step toward accepting his past, an undertaking vital to his achieving a meaningful life.

In order to make this magic more plausible, Wilson provided additional information. In the version developed at the O'Neill Conference, Seth and Bertha have a discussion about the history of their boardinghouse. They review who lived there and when, and remember that Martha Loomis came to the house several years back, seeking Bynum and his binding power to aid in her search for Zonia. The inclusion of this detail supports the idea that it was indeed magic that brought Martha to the house for a second time, now to be reunited with her daughter.

The nature of Bynum's work requires that the people on whom he works his magic ripen so that they will be ready for it. Thus, as Wilson developed the play, he more carefully considered the impact of time on the characters. In the first draft, all of the action takes place in less than one week. Loomis arrives at the house on Saturday morning, sends Selig out to find Martha

Thursday afternoon, and has his reunion when Selig returns with her Friday evening.

By the second draft, the timetable was adjusted so that the play takes place over two weeks. Loomis arrives on the first Saturday and is in the house a full week before he contacts Selig. Then it is not until the following Saturday that Selig returns with Martha. This additional week gives Bynum the opportunity to study the other characters and to work his magic accordingly. Bynum also has the time to recognize Loomis, to bring his song out of him, and to facilitate his salvation.

Bynum and Loomis represent opposite ends of the spectrum in terms of their personal search, but their destinies are intertwined and the interaction between them successfully defines both characters. Although their paths cross several times during the play, the two seminal points for them are the scene in which Bynum lures Loomis into talking about his enslavement by Joe Turner, and the scene at the end of Act I when Bynum guides Loomis through a devastating vision.

One of the most important changes in the script occurred when Wilson switched the order in which these two pivotal Bynum/Loomis scenes occur. In the first drafts of the script, Loomis tells his story in the third scene of Act I, which opens with Seth and Bynum playing dominoes. During the course of this scene, Bynum sings a song he heard in the fields — the lament by women whose men have been captured by Joe Turner. His song attracts Loomis, who stops Bynum's singing and then is encouraged by Bynum to tell the story of his own capture by Joe Turner. Bynum explains to Loomis that he recognizes him as "one of Joe Turner's niggers. 'Cause you forgot how to sing your song."[15] It is at this point in the play that Loomis explains his servitude, his search, and his need for a new beginning. It is also where Bynum reveals the depth of his understanding of Loomis, speaking of the need for Loomis to regain his song, that is, his identity, and take his place in the world.

In the third draft of the script this scene, in which Loomis reveals his past, is moved into the second act. Thus, the full story of Loomis' history with Joe Turner, as told to Bynum, now follows the last scene in Act I, the scene of Loomis' vision. At that point

87

in the play, Loomis finds the other characters doing a juba dance in the kitchen and invoking the holy ghost. He becomes passionate in his condemnation of their devotion to Christian religion, and soon is overtaken by a haunting vision of bones walking on the ocean water. They are the bones of those lost during the middle passage—the travel across the Atlantic into slavery when many Africans either drowned or jumped overboard rather than face enslavement. Loomis sees the bones sink back into the water and then rise up as fully formed men who look like him; he is terrified.

Wilson struggled with this moment in the play and his portrayal of Loomis' inability to reconcile a cultural past he does not acknowledge; while Loomis admits to his personal servitude, he does not recognize the connection he has with those enslaved before him. During the rehearsal process at the Yale Rep, Wilson made a vital revision of the script. In his vision, Loomis sees the bones people stand and walk onto the shore. In previous drafts, Loomis rose with them. In the draft developed at the Yale Rep, Loomis wants to walk with them, but he is unable to stand up. This is a crucial revelation of Loomis' dilemma; he cannot join those on the road. He is unable to accept what the vision is revealing to him—that slavery is his history, too, that these are his people, and that he must acknowledge his past if he is to establish his place in the world and move effectively into the future.

The sense of Loomis' handicap is made more powerful by the reordering of these two crucial scenes. In the first two drafts, Loomis talks about Joe Turner before the bones/vision scene, letting the audience know his history and the depth of his suffering. If we witness Loomis being crippled by his vision before we know his history, the impact becomes much greater because, like Loomis, we are not sure what the vision represents or what message it has to offer; and in our uncertainty, we share the character's confusion and fear. Then, later, when Bynum encourages Loomis to discuss his past and tells Loomis he must find his song in himself and bring it out, we begin to understand at the same time as Loomis begins to understand.

A number of other small changes were made in the two key Bynum/Loomis scenes which help to clarify the quests of these characters. Bynum's search for his Shiney Man does not merely entail waiting for Selig to find him. Nor does it end merely with Loomis' arrival. Rather, Bynum facilitates the finding of his Shiney Man by actually enabling Loomis to shine. In preparation for the O'Neill Conference and in work done while the play was developed there, Wilson gave Bynum a number of lines within the vision scene that strengthen his role as a motivating force for Loomis' eventual catharsis. Bynum actively guides Loomis to the understanding that makes him a Shiney Man.

In the O'Neill draft, Wilson created a call and response rhythm for Bynum. As Loomis describes the bones coming to life, Bynum keeps him moving forward: "Tell me what you seen....What you waiting on, Herald Loomis....What you gonna do now....What you gonna do Herald Loomis?"[16]

In the script for the Yale Rep, Wilson made Bynum an even more effective teacher. Lines were reassigned so that Bynum no longer explains the vision to Loomis, as he had done previously, but rather helps him see it more vividly through the questions he asks. For example, instead of having Bynum tell Loomis the bones sank, Wilson now has Bynum asking Loomis what happened and Loomis replying. Instead of Bynum telling Loomis that the bones with the flesh on them are "...Black. Just like you and me," Loomis now has this line of dialogue.[17]

At the conclusion of the scene, Wilson, again reassigning lines, made an aligned, though seemingly opposite, change. No longer is it Loomis who describes the bones rising up and walking, as he did in the earlier version. Loomis cannot acknowledge this vital final element, so Bynum must be the one to reveal that the "bones people" are standing, and to encourage the crippled Loomis to join them. These changes are important, both for the development of Bynum's character as an instrument of change and for Loomis' progression to his ultimate salvation.

Wilson consistently uses Bynum as the lightening rod for Loomis' electrifying revelations and he continued, through script revisions, to strengthen Bynum's effect on Loomis in small but potent ways. In the first two drafts, when Loomis enters the scene in which he eventually discusses his captivity under Joe Turner, he does so from inside the house; Bynum knows that Loomis is upstairs when he begins to sing several minutes into the scene. In the Yale Rep version, Loomis enters the house from outside, thus suggesting the possibility that Bynum has actually drawn Loomis in with his song.

At the O'Neill Conference, a new section was added in which Bynum leads Loomis to confess that he served Joe Turner. By starting a seemingly innocent discussion about farming that eventually homes in on Loomis' plantation experience, Bynum jump-starts Loomis' story for him by saying, "Joe Turner done caught you."[18] Following that, Wilson made an addition in which Bynum sings another chorus of "Joe Turner," the final key in releasing the history Loomis has denied.

Wilson made another important change at the O'Neill Conference at the point in the play immediately after Bynum identifies Loomis as "one of Joe Turner's niggers."[19] He eliminated Bynum's line to Loomis: "You ain't got to get excited. I ain't meant no harm."[20] For indeed, Bynum did want Loomis to get excited, and Loomis' angry response is all the more powerful in the absence of Bynum's apology. "You lie. How can you see that? I got a mark on me? Joe Turner done marked me to where you can see it? You telling me I'm a marked man? What kind of mark you got on you?"[21]

As Loomis begins to tell his tale, Wilson deleted questions he had earlier assigned to Bynum to assist in the flow of the dialogue: "How you get separated from...this woman you looking for?"[22] Now Loomis is allowed to recount his story without interruption, and the result is a mesmerizing confession.

Up to this point in the play, Loomis' emotional bondage keeps him separated from the other characters. Wilson emphasized this isolation by cutting casual conversations between Loomis and the other boarders. Wilson also had Loomis come and go quickly. Instead of putting Loomis onstage at the beginning of the scene, which would suggest that he has had interaction with someone, Wilson had Loomis enter after the scene is in progress and leave as soon as he can.

Loomis' inability to interact socially results from his loss of identity. But Wilson goes further in revealing the devastating effect enslavement has had on this man. Loomis knows he will not rejoin his wife; he needs a new start. In the initial version of the play, Loomis makes a pass at Molly and takes her up to his room. Before bringing the play to the O'Neill Conference, Wilson changed the object of Loomis' attention to Mattie, who, like Loomis, has never "found no place for [her] to fit in."[23] Because she also needs to reconnect, her pairing with Loomis makes more sense.

In Loomis' encounter with Molly in the first draft, he grabs her and clumsily kisses her. She tries to slow him down and he kisses her again. In later drafts, when Loomis approaches Mattie, "he touches her awkwardly, gently, tenderly. Inside, he howls like a lost wolf pup whose hunger is deep."[24] In the final version of the script, Wilson pulls back even further from the sexuality of the encounter. Loomis no longer says "You got to help me find the soft parts."[25] In fact, the stage direction reads that Loomis cannot reach out to Mattie and he tells her "I done forgot how to touch."[26]

Although Loomis is socially isolated, the script was revised to emphasize his spiritual connection to Bynum. Wilson added to Bynum's Shiney Man speech the fact that Bynum witnessed his vision near the ocean and that it was something "[he] ain't got words to tell you."[27] There is no further description, but it leads to the possibility that Bynum had the same vision as Loomis did.

As Bynum begins to encourage Loomis to reveal his past, Bynum tells a story. In the first two drafts, he spoke in the third person about searching for one's song and how that search binds one to the road. Bynum is indirectly describing Herald Loomis. In the draft developed for the Yale Rep, Wilson modified this speech so that Bynum speaks in the first person, describing his own experience, his own search. This is a much more powerful choice as Bynum recognizes himself as akin to Loomis and opens the door for Loomis to reciprocate. It also suggests how Bynum knows so much about Loomis and why he can serve as an agent in Loomis' self healing. At the end of the play, Bynum challenges Loomis to stand, as he himself has done: "You bound onto your song. All you got to do is stand and sing it, Herald Loomis. It's right there kicking at your throat. All you got to do is sing it. Then you be free."[28]

In all of Loomis' interactions with Bynum, Wilson worked to

clarify Loomis' progress toward his salvation at the end of the play
— salvation which comes from recognition and acceptance of
one's personal and cultural past. Loomis must acknowledge the
history of his people. In the draft developed at the O'Neill
Conference, Loomis begins by connecting his past with that of
Bynum. Although Bynum was not held by Joe Turner, he has
accepted and carries within himself the enslavement of his ancestors. Loomis says to him, "You one of them Bones people."[29]

Loomis also needs to acknowledge his own point of origin
before he can begin his new journey. Although he cannot return
to a life left long behind, he must revisit it so that he can move
forward. When Loomis sees his wife, and passes to her the daughter for whom he has cared, he can begin to unbind himself from
the road and all else that tethers him. At the end of the play,
Loomis pulls out a knife and holds it to his chest.

As Martha (who has been born again and taken the surname
Pentecost) preaches to her husband from the Bible, Loomis
takes his final steps to freedom. While working at the O'Neill
Conference, Wilson added lines that specify Loomis' action as the
most vital personal salvation.

> **MARTHA:** The blood of Jesus, Herald. It'll wash you clean.
>
> **LOOMIS:** Blood make you clean? You clean with blood?
>
> **MARTHA:** Jesus bled for you....
>
> **LOOMIS:** I don't need nobody to bleed for me. I can bleed for
> myself.[30]

Loomis takes responsibility for himself and slashes his chest — a
transcendental act which recalls the action of Bynum's Shiney Man.

It is after Loomis rubs himself with his blood and then exits
through the door that Bynum sees him shine. Wilson's final stage
direction describes the freedom Loomis has achieved:

> Having found his song, the song of self-sufficiency, fully resur-
> rected, cleansed and given breath, free from any encumbrance
> other than the workings of his own heart and the bonds of the
> flesh, having accepted responsibility for his own presence in the

world, he is free to soar above the environs that weighed and pushed his spirit into terrifying contractions.[31]

Joe Turner's Come and Gone is Wilson's favorite of his plays.

> My favorite part is the story of the bones. I felt so complete after I wrote it. I had taken the bones of the Africans who were thrown overboard during the Middle Passage and symbolically resurrected them. I had marched them across the water and upon the land and connected them with the Africans who are in America now. I said to myself then, "If I die tomorrow, I have fulfilled myself as an artist."[32]

Joe Turner is Wilson's most spiritual play, trading in what the theater does best—gathering people together and creating magic and ceremony. Through the years of its development, the play became significantly more mystical and more potent. The incorporation of mysticism into *Joe Turner's Come and Gone* was as extraordinary an effort for Wilson as it was for his characters, a means for both playwright and players to reexamine the past and bring it into the present. The result is a compelling drama that poetically expresses a powerful message. No one can escape the past. Buried deep in each person is history. To search for this history, and to accept it, is life's most important journey, for only through this journey can one achieve an understanding of oneself.

The Final Knockout

August Wilson at the Yale Repertory Theatre and on the Road to Broadway

From the beginning, August Wilson associated the process of refining his plays with Lloyd Richards, who was, when Wilson first met him, Artistic Director of both the Eugene O'Neill Theater Center and the Yale Repertory Theatre. The two men bonded immediately, creatively and personally. Wilson is driven by the need to award the African-American experience its deserved place in history and on stage. He feels that "the black experience has no historical weight in American history. I try simply to restore the experience to a primary position, showing a world in which the black American was the spiritual center."[1] Richards feels the same obligation.

> The black people [are] a disinherited nation, stripped of their lands and put into servitude in another land, where their culture was not so much a matter of choice but imposition. You'll find very little on the bookshelves, in the literature of the theater, that speaks of this. Theater is the place where I work. It is my life. It is part of my responsibility to address those shelves, the gaps on those shelves, so that the work continues to expand.[2]

It was Richards who brought Wilson's work to the Yale Rep. *Ma Rainey's Black Bottom, Fences, Joe Turner's Come and Gone, The Piano Lesson*, and *Two Trains Running* were all produced there. Wilson feels artistically connected with Richards: "Our visions are the same. We come from the same place. I trust Lloyd's understanding of the characters."[3] Wilson also respects Richards' values and priorities. He recalls the moment when they first met to discuss production of *Ma Rainey's Black Bottom*:

> When I first met Lloyd he looked at me very seriously and said, "You've got a lot of work to do," and I said, "I ain't never been scared of hard work." Then he changed the subject completely and he told me that raising his kid was the single most important accomplishment of his life. That told me the kind of person he was.[4]

Gitta Honegger was the resident dramaturg at the Yale Rep when Wilson worked there. She admired what she describes as "an extremely trusting working relationship [between Wilson and Richards]. A cliche would be father and son, but that was the feeling."[5] Wilson agrees.

> I'm a great boxing fan, and boxing is like writing. I look at Lloyd like he's my trainer. Now, Lloyd is old enough to be my father. Having grown up without a father, that has a lot to do with my relationship with him. I always view him in a fatherly way. You know, you want to please Pop. You want Pop to be proud of you. I want to score a knockout.[6]

Richards' artistic vision has impacted on all of Wilson's plays. At times, his comments were general, concerning, for example, the length of a play. Other times, he would specifically question a speech given by a character which he felt was inconsistent with Wilson's overall portrayal. In the case of *Two Trains Running*, Richards suggested changing the year in which the play was set. Wilson had originally set the play in 1968. Richards wanted to push it later since the play does not address Martin Luther King's assassination. The final version of the play is set in 1969.

In speaking of their work, Richards says it is difficult to remember who first suggested a change:

> When you're working as closely as we were, the interesting thing is that you can't identify all of [the changes]. I mean you can't identify whether I said it or whether August said it. Because you're working together and you come to a conclusion and the conclusion is the choice. And whether I suggested, "do this" or he said, "I'm going to do this!" is almost insignificant. You get that close together that you function, really, two entities as one person — just two entities of the creation and of the creative act. [7]

Over the course of five plays and thirteen years, Richards taught Wilson a great deal about the professional theater. They first met at the O'Neill Conference in 1982. They formed their partnership in 1984, when rehearsals for *Ma Rainey's Black Bottom* began at the Yale Rep. Wilson admits he knew very little about theatrical production at that time.

> I discovered I didn't know anything about casting. I remember the first audition for *Ma Rainey*, I was ready to hire anybody who could read. So Lloyd cast it. The first day of rehearsal the actors read the script and they had some questions. Before I could get it together, Lloyd started answering the questions. And he knew the answers. I found out that he knew the characters like I did.

> He included me in everything that happened. He would say, "They are building the set over there in the shop. Did you stop by and see what they are doing?" I said no. He said, "Why don't you stop by?" He wanted me to know how it happened, that it didn't just come from nowhere. [8]

Richards, a veteran theater director, enjoyed working with Wilson, the poet turned playwright. But Wilson's lack of experience with "theatrical rules" became problematic for Richards, who urged

Wilson to make major revisions to create a more traditional underlying structure for his play.

> August was a fast learner. There was the very marvelous, unique storytelling capacity of this writer, and his uncanny ability to perceive characters and to illuminate them through storytelling. But he had to begin to learn to dramatize. Then you learn other old tricks along the way, and one of the reasons that I very seldom talk to August about craft is because you can get locked into craft and stifle his creative impulse.
>
> August was not an experienced playwright.... He'd written a couple of plays. He hadn't had a lot of production. And our work became, very much, finding the line, the structure, the spine of the play. And then pulling that spine through the material. The very simple fact is that he is a poet, and a poet does not write a dramatic story line. But we took the problem at hand, to make a dramatic event out of the material. It was a matter of really finding the thing that began to shape the play, that put a spine in the play. I would ask him questions, and he would dig for the answers and come up with them. And through that process we structured a play out of what were very marvelous characters and wonderful events and great storytelling. We tried to evolve a dramatic structure through that. That's been true in most of the plays.[9]

Thus, when Wilson and Richards worked together, Richards' focus was clearly on restructuring the plays. As he describes it, "our work consists of sorting through the mystical material and rearranging it so that it becomes useful."[10]

> Things were put in different places and things fell away. August was very, very good about that. Not good about it in that he was giving in to something but good in his ability to perceive the questions that were being asked and to respond to them in terms of those questions, creating new adjustments, rewriting or whatever.[11]

And Wilson agrees that a new arrangement of the same material may sometimes be more evocative:

> With most plays I have a good idea of what it is that I want to do and so then I try to determine: if I'm saying it this way is the audience hearing it and understanding it and, if not, what can be done to clarify it. The whole thing is about clarity. If you have a lot of good material but the audience doesn't understand it, then you're defeating your own purpose. It should be clear to the audience. And a lot of time making it clear is simply that you have something in the wrong place. Putting it in another place makes them say, "Oh, I can see that now." It focuses things and removes things blocking your way.[12]

Those who witnessed their collaboration acknowledge Richards' dramaturgical focus and its resultant impact on Wilson. Gitta Honegger says, "Lloyd does know how things pay off; how you set them up."[13] Even the actors recognize Richard's impact on the work; Charles Dutton who appeared in the premier productions of *Ma Rainey*, *Joe Turner's Come and Gone*, and *Piano Lesson* believes Richards is largely responsible for the structural changes.

> Anything where you actually talk about moving something structurally, a lot of that input would come from Lloyd Richards. If it's one thing that Lloyd is an expert in, it is the way a play should move. And August listens, intently, to Lloyd's suggestions.[14]

But restructuring was also an ongoing battle, as Wilson continued to give precedence to his characterizations and to protect his signature storytelling. Charles Dutton recognized the seeds of the conflict.

> August basically writes. I mean, he doesn't concern himself at the outset with a structure and your standard 101 Playwriting technique. August just comes up with the characters and just lets the characters talk. Through the dialogue and through the

characters' exploration of who they are, the structure comes
organically. Most of his original drafts are way too long. I mean
some of August's characters can talk seven, eight pages. And all
of his plays take that shape because August doesn't limit himself.
He just lets the plays run for as long as they like to. And that's
the beauty of it.[15]

Not everyone immediately saw the beauty of the long stories. And
despite the cutting which had been done at the O'Neill
Conference, there was concern at the Yale Rep that *Ma Rainey's
Black Bottom* was still too long. Kim Powers, a Yale Drama School
dramaturgy student who was assigned to the play as production
dramaturg, recalls:

What had become the characteristic of August was these long
storytelling riffs he goes off on. These sort of poetic, lyrical
things that at times don't necessarily even seem connected to
the play. That was the biggest concern I had and I think several
people had. Were they going to work? And that was the thing
I was constantly after, not cutting them completely but trimming
them and trying to integrate them in a fuller way.[16]

But Powers ran into opposition, not only from Wilson but also
from Richards who himself was trying to balance his preference
for traditional structure with his recognition of Wilson's unique
voice.

In the end, it was accepted that Wilson's extraordinary stories
could work dramatically if they were moderated through cuts and
revisions. Other unorthodox elements of the play, however,
remained problematic and Richards continually had to overcome
difficulties created by an impractical playwright.

A part of the playwright's lack of awareness in *Ma Rainey* is —
and I never said this to August — if you're a smart playwright you
do not write six characters in a play who are accomplished musicians who have to play onstage. Okay, you've written yourself
into a lot of problems. Now those were problems that I had to

deal with. I would not say, "August, you don't do that!" Or "one doesn't do that." I didn't try and teach him playwriting. I would work and dramatize.[17]

Richards felt that part of helping Wilson "dramatize" was encouraging the efforts of the poet who was teaching himself to write dialogue. In the process of doing so, Wilson proved willing to follow suggestions not only from Richards but from the actors with whom he worked. The draft of *Ma Rainey's Black Bottom* that Wilson brought to the Yale Rep included a line supplied by an actor at the O'Neill — the young man playing the policeman who escorts Ma to the recording session. He told Wilson that his dialogue was not authentic to a Chicago cop. Wilson challenged him to write a new line. The actor offered, "Look, buddy, you want it in a nutshell, we got her charged with assault and battery." Wilson later included these words in the play.

Wilson's poetry background created one final hurdle for Richards as he worked on *Ma Rainey*.

The imagery of a poet is different from the imagery of a playwright, because a playwright sees a play happening in space. In August's initial work, space was absent, and when I brought space into it, just in terms of the definition of sets, that had not been part of his craft.[18]

In 1985, Richards and Wilson reunited for the production of *Fences*. Again Richards ran into practical problems when he began to stage this play.

What would happen very often is the person who ended a scene would start the next scene, and it might be a day later. Once it's six months later. You're always working in the theater. There's very little time between scenes. And if you end a scene with one person and you're starting the next scene six months later with the same person — and the first one has a very dramatic conclusion — and the next scene is a very different emotional attitude, then what you've got in that time — and you have less than ten seconds to do it — or you want less than ten seconds to do it — is you have to change the scene, you have to change the costumes, and the actor has to make that leap, that emotional leap. Now, an experienced playwright would know better than to do that. He'd bring him in a page later, or you find a way. So in *Fences* we even had to find the ways to do those things, because that wasn't a part of the playwright's awareness.[19]

But Richards' input was not exclusively practical or structural. He also influenced the development of the characters. At the end of Act I in the version of *Fences* that Wilson brought to the Yale Rep, the central character, Troy, rails against God for denying him the rewards of his years of service. In an early rehearsal, Richards told Wilson he didn't believe Troy had a relationship with God. "Troy's line in that play was very important to the development of the structure of the play. And it suddenly occurred to me that that was one of the flaws in Troy's lines."[20] Wilson concurred, but remarked that Troy surely did have a relationship with death. So he replaced Troy's original speech to God with a challenge to Mr. Death to try and come for him. The rewritten speech opened the door to Richards' ultimate approach to directing the play. "It was the restructuring of that speech, from a speech to God to a speech to Death...that made it possible for us to then take that and develop the core of the play. That was the key to *Fences*."[21] It was central to Troy's definition of responsibility.

In the version of *Fences* produced at the Yale Rep, Death finally comes and wins his battle with Troy, and the play ends with Troy's family preparing for his funeral. Since the final scene is set several years after the preceding scenes, it paved the way for Richards to open a discussion about restructuring the play.

> *Fences* is an interesting mixture because *Fences* can be looked at or presented as a flashback. You can start *Fences* with the last scene and do the rest of the play in flashback. We discussed that. And the fact is that it is a flashback without being a flashback. It is a play about the effect of that man on his family.[22]

Some have suggested that Richards was drawn to having Wilson reformat the play in flashback mode in order to satisfy James Earl Jones, the star playing Troy. Jones was unhappy that his character, dead by then, did not appear in the last scene. Richards admits there was tension.

> It's very difficult to give a star a lead in a play and say, "You're not on stage for the last scene." It was very tough for Jimmy. There were a few things that were tough for Jimmy, but that's the play. We could have chosen to accommodate a star — we could have started the play with the last scene. There were several things we could have done to accommodate the actor. And those were certainly part of the decisions that were made. We dealt with that question, August and I. We had alternatives or we could proceed with it the way it was and we made a decision. [23]

At the time, Richards did not remember that Wilson's first draft of the play had indeed been written with most of the play's action as flashback. But following work at the O'Neill Pre-Conference, Wilson had abandoned this form and, when Richards mentioned it again during rehearsals at Yale Rep, Wilson stuck to his previous decision against it.

Wilson had written *Fences* with James Earl Jones in mind for the central role. He met Jones shortly after he completed the play while the actor was on tour with Athol Fugard's *Master Harold and the Boys*. Wilson's friend, Claude Purdy, encouraged Wilson to approach him. But Jones' only response to the young playwright who had written a play for him was "good luck with it." [24] Ultimately, he agreed to perform in the play, but he was never satisfied with it.

> August does not necessarily end a play; he is almost reluctant to end a play because he has this great energy. I was actively critical of the lack of resolution in *Fences*. As an artist within a drama, I could not appreciate this. Perhaps as an outsider it would have been different. [25]

Wilson's interaction with the actors, which was often moderated by Richards, involved issues as general as the play's conclusion and as specific as individual lines. Mary Alice, who portrayed the character of Rose in *Fences*, remembers that Wilson was always willing to listen, although not always willing to comply.

> I felt he was always open to listening to the actors, but I also real-
> ized that he was very firm on what he wanted. For example, I
> had some reservations about playing a line. This is in the scene
> when Troy brings the baby home to Rose to be the baby's
> mother, and there's a line at the end of that scene: "From right
> now, this child's got a mother; but you a womanless man." I
> really didn't want to say, "You a womanless man." And I
> remember talking to August about it and talking to Lloyd about
> it. I just didn't want to say that line, and August, of course, want-
> ed that spoken just as it was written. And, of course, after I did
> it I realized why. Because the audience responded to that so
> viscerally.[26]

James Earl Jones also complained about the same line but he did so because of the visceral response it generated. He felt that it encouraged the audience to dislike his character. It was Richards who convinced him that, in fact, the scene created sympathy for Troy.

As the play progressed from its production at the Yale Rep to commercial productions in San Francisco and on Broadway, Jones continued to push for changes. In one instance, Wilson did change a line, or rather add a line, at the suggestion of Jones. Wilson considers it exemplary of an open mind.

> I don't have a problem with people wanting different lines.
> Some of the changes that James Earl wanted were cool, they
> were good, I have to admit. One change was indicative of how
> one line can mean so much, because it can change so much.[27]

Late in *Fences*, Rose accuses Troy of having had his brother, Gabriel, committed. She says she has seen the papers Troy signed when he went down to the courthouse to get Gabriel out of jail, papers in which Troy agreed to have Gabriel placed in a mental hospital. Jones felt the audience could not follow how the action had come to take place. Wilson listened to Jones' point of view and considered his position:

> There was some confusion about the play regarding whether Troy had signed his brother into the hospital or not. In my mind it was like he wanted to get his brother out of jail, so when they said sign here and gimme the fifty dollars, he signed right here. But really that paper was to commit Gabe to a mental hospital, and Troy signs unknowingly, because the last thing he would have done was to sign these papers.
>
> The audience never got that. They asked, "Did he sign it? Or would he sign it? Did he sign it to put him in the hospital?" And James Earl had a problem with this, and I was saying, "Well, look, Troy can't read. So, therefore, you know, he just signed the thing, he don't know what it said, right?" So, [James Earl] said, "Why can't I say I can't read." I said, "Because Troy would never admit that to nobody."
>
> I had a very nice lunch with James Earl and he had a couple of things that we addressed and that came up again He said, "Can I say I can't read tonight?" I said, "Yeah, okay, say you can't read." Well, that scene came up and it worked. I heard it.
>
> I was up in the balcony somewhere, and I heard it. And it was the first time in my life I heard those words. And he's big and he says, "Aw hell, you know I can't read." And it was like, wow. And I think it suddenly became clear. And I ran to him and I said, "Keep it. Keep it. Keep it. Say it just like that." "Aw hell, you know I can't read." See, he made it real.
>
> I didn't go over and say I'm not gonna put that in there because I didn't write it and whatever I write is set in stone. I reserve the right to take his suggestions.[28]

And, similarly, Wilson reserved the right not to make changes, whether they were suggested by Jones or by the play's commercial producer, Carol Shorenstein Hays.[29] Hays, like Jones, or perhaps because of Jones, was unhappy with the ending of the play. In the final moments of *Fences*, Gabriel tries to blow his trumpet to open the gates of heaven so that Troy can enter. Unable to get the instrument to work, Gabriel completes his task by performing a short dance and using his own vocal strength to announce his brother's arrival in heaven. Relieved that he did not fail in his efforts, Gabriel closes the play by saying "That's how that go." Hays hated the line and suggested Gabriel say "Hallelujah" instead. Wilson did not agree.

> James Earl wasn't satisfied with the ending. He was dissatisfied with the whole scene. And Carol became dissatisfied with Gabriel coming in at the end and blowing the trumpet and saying, "That's the way that go." To her, see, that was like, "That's all folks!" The Warner Brothers saying, "That's all folks."
>
> She was trying to keep the audience from laughing at the end. And I thought after going through all that, watching Gabe go through all that, because it was very anguishing to watch this man try to blow the horn and have it not work. The horn that man's been carrying around twenty years waiting to blow does not work. I mean, what do you do? Some people went through that anguish with him, so when he makes the horn noise himself and says "That's how that go," you laugh.
>
> You had a release—now you're ready to applaud, you feel good. So you don't end up in anguish, right? And "Hallelujah" and stopping that laugh is not going to work. You want that laugh. And that's what I tried to explain to her. You gotta have the audience laugh. She said, "Well it's like, That's all, folks! The Bugs Bunny thing."
>
> It is the choice of the playwright that got you up there to the

end, and if you got the audience to the end, then you get to call the shots. That's the way I feel. Since I got it all the way there, I should have the last say and I didn't want hallelujah. That didn't say anything. "That's the way that go" puts a cap on it. That's the way that story goes. That's how you do that. And, you know, there's a wealth of things in here.[30]

Hays continued to dislike the closing line and also wanted other changes to which Wilson objected. Shortly before *Fences'* Broadway opening, tensions that had been building came to a head. Unable to convince Wilson to make the changes and unable to convince Richards to force Wilson to make the changes, Hays called the entire cast and crew together early on the Saturday morning before the play was to open and announced that she had fired Lloyd Richards.

There was speculation that Hays had in mind replacing Richards with James Earl Jones. Many felt that what Hays was requesting, ultimately only a change in a line of dialogue and a modified action at the end of the play, reflected Jones' creative input. The meeting ended abruptly with Wilson storming out. Shortly thereafter, his lawyers informed Hays that any changes made without Wilson's approval would be in violation of his contract.

By Saturday evening, their lawyers, fearing for the future of the production, had convinced Wilson and Hays to sit down together to discuss their differences. Wilson agreed to allow a matinee performance the following day which included the changes Hays had proposed. But he reserved the right to reject them after the trial performance.

Wilson watched the show and was pained by the final moments of his work. But he was not alone. Immediately after the show, Hays told Wilson she preferred to leave *Fences* as he had written it. Richards was reinstated.

It is rumored, although not confirmed, that when Wilson began production of *Joe Turner's Come and Gone* his contract specifically denied producers the opportunity to have creative input into the production. Lloyd Richards, however, continued to be an active and welcome participant.

As rehearsals of *Joe Turner's Come and Gone* began at the Yale Rep, Richards was concerned once again with the number of stories told in the play. *Ma Rainey's Black Bottom* had proven that there was room for a great quantity of storytelling, but Wilson remembers that Richards felt the play needed trimming:

> Lloyd has a unique way of making suggestions. One day he came to me and said. "I think you have one too many stories in this play. See what you can do with that." So I went away and when I came to rehearsal the next day Lloyd said to me, "Did you make any changes?" I told him no, I couldn't find anything to cut. So then he said "I think you need to look at that again." So I looked at the play which had one story and then another story and then another story so I just picked the one that I thought that I could live without, and cut it. [31]

Richards remembers the event with amusement:

> I said to him at one point, "You know, there's one scene too many," And I handed him back the script. And so he went and pored over the script, and finally he found the scene that he eliminated and he brought it back and gave it to me and I went on working on it. Well, he doesn't know to this day whether he eliminated the same scene that I was speaking of. [32]

But Wilson knew that if he had cut a speech Richards considered important, his director would have let him know.

As each of Wilson's plays approached commercial production, there was always external pressure to shorten the work to a more conventional two and one-half hour playing time. Richards was not always responsive and argued, "I find that a sad concept. Does that rule apply to *The Merchant of Venice*? I hear it runs more than three hours. Has anybody spoken to Mr. Shakespeare lately about doing something about it?" [33] Wilson agrees. "I don't think there should be an arbitrarily-set running time for a play. If it takes three hours to tell a particular story, it takes three hours to tell a story."[34] And some people who know what was cut miss the deleted material. Charles Dutton remembers:

> I saw in all of his plays, *Ma Rainey, Joe Turner, Piano Lesson,* where he's basically had to cut another play out of the play. You know? I miss some things. Some days, on my television show [Roc], I'd sit around with Carl Gordon and Rocky Carol, who were in *The Piano Lesson* with me, and we'd simply recite lines that were cut out of *Piano Lesson* that were great lines and passages and pages that didn't make it into the play. And I'd say, "Do you remember that one?" And I'd recite him some stuff, and he'd say, "Oh, I forgot that one. Do you remember this one?" And so, August leaves a lot of plays on the floor when he's writing them, you know, on the cutting floor.[35]

Often, the cuts suggested by Richards had nothing to do with overall playing time but instead were intended to clarify the story line or heighten the drama. Early in the draft of *Joe Turner* that Wilson brought to the Yale Rep, in a scene between Zonia and Reuben, Zonia describes her father's plan of action should he find his wife. Wilson remembers a specific change requested by Richards.

> Reuben says, "What's he gonna do when he find her?" And Zonia says, "Tell her good-bye." And I remember Lloyd saying, "Why do you have the kid giving it away that he's going to tell her good-bye? Because the audience thinks that they're going to reconcile. So you shouldn't have the kid say he's looking for her to tell her good-bye." I thought, "Yeah, that makes sense." So that was one of the changes I know I got from Lloyd. That made a big difference.[36]

Richards also pointed out places in which he thought something was missing from the script. Such was the case with the scene at the end of Act I of *Joe Turner* in which Loomis has his vision. Richards' complaint is still fresh in Wilson's mind:

I remember in rehearsal Lloyd kept saying, "You have to see the moment where Loomis finds his song." And I said, "Yeah, Lloyd. Tell me what else is new. Of course you have to see that moment where Loomis finds his song. How to show that I have no idea," I didn't have any idea. He said, "Keep working on it." I said, "I'll keep working." We solved it and somehow I came up with his being unable to stand and then it made sense.[37]

The focus of Richards' work was always to provide a more accessible, more literal script. David Moore, the production dramaturg for the Yale Rep production of *Joe Turner*, would have opted for another approach.

August and I had a couple of very long conversations about his other work, and other ways, strategically, to approach *Joe Turner* in terms of a world to create on the stage. And we talked about a "what if?" The idea that if the play were not treated literally and what would that imply for his writing? And what would it imply if the script weren't changed at all? Lloyd's production was solid, naturalistic, etc. And I'll just say we talked a lot, always very respectful of Lloyd, we talked a lot about non-literal ways of interpreting the play for staging.[38]

But the creative work on the script was clearly the exclusive domain of the playwright and the director. Moore remembers the process between Richards and Wilson as relatively closed to input from others.

You're talking a very private artist in the way that Lloyd works. Neither of these guys are big speech makers; and neither of them are terribly big on pulling the team into a circle and openly discussing stuff. So it was very warm and friendly but it was a very craft-oriented, straight-ahead production process.[39]

Dramaturg Gitta Honegger had a similar experience. Although she had many discussions with Wilson about his plays, she found

110

she had a limited role in the process of revision.

> It was such a generous atmosphere in the rehearsal hall. We all
> had a really jovial, joking, wonderful open relationship, so that
> there was just an interaction. But Lloyd was the one who dis-
> cussed the text and there was never a question about that, that
> was clear— it was Lloyd and August. As much as I say it was a
> very generous atmosphere, Lloyd was very protective in his rela-
> tionship with August, and Lloyd knew, very clearly, what he
> wanted. And there was no question but that [what Lloyd want-
> ed] was what was going to be done.[40]

Richards also kept the actors at something of a remove from
Wilson. Even though the playwright became progressively more
comfortable with the production process, in 1989, when he and
Richards reunited to work on *The Piano Lesson*, Richards continued to have all of the primary interaction with the actors.
Richards believes that he and Wilson should each do what he
does best.

> I don't go and sit over his shoulder when he sits down to type.
> That's where he does his creative work and I let him do it. And
> I deal with it later. And I work with the actors, that's where I do
> my creative work and he deals with it after.[41]

Richards also believes that he and Wilson, by sharing a vision of
the world, reduce the need for extensive dialogue between them.

> We don't have a lot of discussions; we don't need a lot. I say a
> few things: he understands what I'm talking about. He says
> something: I understand what he's talking about. And we could
> go around the corner on it. That's part of what makes up our
> working relationship.

> There is an affinity of experience and attitude that we share, and
> it has been there through all of our work....The things that

August's characters say, which are articulations of principle, codes of living, attitudes toward their own destiny, visions and images, are things that I understand so that when a character articulates something, I seem to know what is on August's mind. I seldom have to ask, what do you mean by this?[42]

Richards thinks of himself as a facilitator. His stated aim is to support, extend, and supplement Wilson's creative aims. He hopes to illuminate the playwright's work, not impose his vision upon it.

There has been tension and disagreement in their collaboration, acknowledged by both men but rarely discussed publicly; but they have continued to work together. Their creative partnership aside, Wilson recognizes that Richards has contributed greatly to his success by championing his work.

Richards was slated to direct the premier production of *Seven Guitars* at The Goodman Theatre. Emergency surgery forced him to return to New York and he was replaced by Walter Dallas. The production was successful, but when it continued on its road to other regional theaters and to Broadway, Wilson brought Richards back to the production. However, his experience with Dallas had sparked new ideas about his work and his process of playwriting — ideas that continued to develop with Wilson's next production, *Jitney* — and ideas that Wilson feels are continuing to reverberate in the work he does today.

Jitney

August Wilson's
Round Trip

Over the course of less than two decades, August Wilson has grown from a struggling playwright to a consistent and influential voice in the American theatre. His goal is to chronicle this century by setting each of his plays in a different decade. The recent production of *Jitney*, set in 1971, constitutes another chapter in that epic, and the one closest to the present. But *Jitney* is not Wilson's newest work. It was first written in 1979, and the changes he has made to it since then, first in a production at the Pittsburgh Public Theater (spring, 1996), and, most recently, at the Crossroads Theatre in New Brunswick, N.J. (spring, 1997), constitute a chronicle of Wilson's own development, as one of America's most important playwrights reshapes the work of his youth.

The changes Wilson made to *Jitney* reflected a new methodology of playwriting—specifically of rewriting—which he had developed while working on *Seven Guitars* at the Goodman Theatre in Chicago in 1995. Wilson now does all of his rewriting during the rehearsal process, in close collaboration with the director, and inspired by the art, life, and response of the actors.

Unlike the way he revised his previous plays, Wilson barely touched the structure of *Jitney*, adding only one scene to the play.

Instead, he focused on the creation of much richer portraits of his characters, which he accomplished by illuminating the details of their lives and increasing the complexity of their relationships with one another, and by using his gift for language to render the extraordinary pulse of their speech.

The first draft of *Jitney* (1979) exhibits the insecurities of an inexperienced writer—repetition, glaring emotional signposts for the audience, inconsistent dialogue, and an obscure central conflict. Many of the problems were the result, or sometimes the cause, of shallow characterization. When Wilson returned to *Jitney*, he brought with him those qualities that have become his signature as a playwright—a highly-developed instinct for rhythm, nuance, and pacing—and extensive use of storytelling, all in the service of character exploration and the portrayal of the dramatic confrontations inherent in the day-to-day struggle of living.

Wilson was inspired to write *Jitney* during a visit to his hometown of Pittsburgh. One day, he hailed a jitney, a cab that operates in neighborhoods where traditional taxis do not venture, and was struck by the energy of the people who run these car services:

> These guys would just get an abandoned storefront and put a pay phone in there and disseminate the number throughout the community and go into business, thereby creating something out of nothing. These were guys who sent their kids to college driving jitneys.[1]

Wilson returned home, and within ten days had written his play.

Jitney tells the story of five of the men who drive the jitneys. Their station is owned by Becker who holds these men together while struggling with his estrangement from his son, Booster, who was imprisoned for murder twenty-five years earlier. During the course of the play, Booster is released. But his father's sudden death shortly thereafter negates the possibility of any reconciliation between the two men.

The jitney drivers span thirty years in age and experiences that include war, alcoholism, lost love, skirmishes with the law, and continued disappointment. They are Turnbo, a bitter man who fills

his days with a running ironic commentary on the lives of his colleagues, and his favorite target, Youngblood, a twenty-four-year-old
Vietnam veteran who is trying to build a life for his family.
Youngblood's energy contrasts with the resignation of Fielding, a
drinker who still dreams of his wife, dead twenty-two years. The
fourth driver is Doub, a steady worker who remains optimistic
despite the battles he has fought in and out of war. Joining these
men is Shealy, a numbers runner who uses the station as his office.
Day after day, the drivers fan out into the neighborhood to pick up
their fares as they have done for years, only to learn, during the
course of the play, that they will soon face the closing of the station and the loss of their livelihoods.

The original version of *Jitney* represented a significant step in
the development of Wilson's dramaturgy, and the Playwrights
Center in St. Paul, Minnesota, awarded Wilson a fellowship on the
basis of the script. For the first time, he was encouraged to think
of himself a playwright. But national recognition was not readily
forthcoming, and *Jitney* was swiftly rejected by the O'Neill
Playwrights Conference. So Wilson decided to begin a new play
and he put *Jitney* away in a drawer. However, a friend, director Bob
Johnson, asked for a copy to submit to Pittsburgh's Allegheny
Repertory Theatre, which Wilson describes as "six or seven people who had just gotten out of school."[2]

This young theatre presented *Jitney* in 1982 as the final play of
its first season and the hometown response was strong. *Jitney* was
the first play written by a black writer and containing exclusively
black characters to be reviewed by the major Pittsburgh newspapers — the *Pittsburgh Post Gazette* and the *Pittsburgh Press*. The
reviews were generally positive, helping to legitimize the production in both the black and white communities. *Jitney* played to
sold-out houses for the duration of its run. But when Wilson had
no follow-up offers for production, the play went back into the
drawer.

Three years later, Wilson's friend, director Claude Purdy,
chose to mount *Jitney* again. And so, in 1985, Wilson had the
opportunity to revisit the play when it was produced at the
Penumbra Theatre in St. Paul, Minnesota. He considered rewriting the play, but instead decided to "just leave it."[3] In retrospect,

Wilson admits he took the easy way out. At that time, he had two plays in production, *Ma Rainey's Black Bottom* on Broadway and *Fences* at the Yale Repertory Theatre. Although he had done extensive rewrites on both plays during the process of their development, he had been assisted in this by workshops at the O'Neill Center, sophisticated dramaturgs, and a close collaboration with Lloyd Richards. With *Jitney*, Wilson would have had to go it alone, a prospect he found overwhelming since, as he says, "I had no idea how to rewrite that play."⁴ So, it was performed unchanged.

Eleven more years had passed when Edward Gilbert, Artistic Director of The Pittsburgh Public Theater, asked to read the play. He soon scheduled *Jitney* for June 1996 production. With four major plays behind him, Wilson now felt secure in his ability to rewrite. Still, he did not even reread the script before it began rehearsal in Pittsburgh. His choice not to work on the play before production did not indicate his satisfaction with the script; on the contrary, Wilson had been aware for years of the play's deficiencies. Nor, this time, did it reflect apprehension about the rewriting process. Rather, having recently discovered what he believes to be the most productive approach to revising his work, Wilson made a conscious choice to wait until rehearsals began.

Until *Seven Guitars*, Wilson had done the major rewrites of his first drafts before the shows began rehearsal for their premiere productions, which took place most often at the Yale Rep Theatre. As the plays moved from regional theater to regional theater, en route to Broadway, he did additional work on them alone, and submitted the revised drafts before rehearsal began. During rehearsal, he made what he terms "minor adjustments." This was the process that resulted in the highly successful productions of *Ma Rainey's Black Bottom, Fences, Joe Turner's Come and Gone, The Piano Lesson,* and *Two Trains Running*.

Wilson had intended to follow the same route to revisions with *Seven Guitars*. But thanks to his tendency to procrastinate, he discovered a new process.

> With *Seven Guitars* I had never rewritten the play from its first draft. I think I meant to rewrite it but I never could, I never got to it. So I just said, "Ah, I'll do it in rehearsal." And I discovered

a new way of working and that is working in the heat of the
moment, in rehearsal, doing the rewrites. You're writing on the
spot, as opposed to writing at home and coming in with the
script and making small changes. But it turned out to be fruit-
ful, I think, so I decided to do it again with *Jitney*.[5]

No doubt Wilson's new process was occasioned, at least partially,
by the absence of his mentor, Lloyd Richards, who was hospital-
ized in New York when *Seven Guitars* began production in
Chicago. From the outset, Wilson worked differently with
Richards' successor, Walter Dallas, forming a much more collaborative, egalitarian partnership. They discussed the script extensively, and Wilson appreciated the give-and-take.

Lloyd doesn't do a lot of talking so you can't talk over ideas and
concepts and things with Lloyd. You just kind of go over here
and do your work and say "Lloyd here's what I did" and he says
"OK" and he does it. Sometimes he doesn't even question it.
Walter talks specifically about the work, so it's very interesting
to work with him. The primary difference is that I talk a lot more
than I did with Lloyd.[6]

For his part, Dallas feels a certain pride in his role in the development of Wilson's new process:

I think when we worked together on *Seven Guitars* it changed
how he worked. And that's how he works now. We're in the
moment, we're in the rehearsals and we talk to each other during, between, after, before, sometimes directly about what's
onstage or maybe more generally about that world surrounding
what's happening onstage.[7]

The inspiration for this process may lie in the fact that both men
had experienced something similar while working at the O'Neill
Center, a high-pressure but critic-free environment where playwrights quickly and instinctively revise their plays during a short
rehearsal process. Wilson had enjoyed the challenge within the

relatively secure world of the O'Neill, but had lacked the confidence to try to produce new material on the spot when his plays moved into regional theaters. Now more sure of himself, Wilson enjoys the immediacy of rewriting during rehearsals. Dallas supports the approach:

> It really works to get in a room with the playwright. Most of the dramaturgical work we'd just come up with in rehearsal—things that make a difference. Sometimes I hear them, sometimes August hears them. And then he just makes the change. He make those changes there rather than going off to his room and coming back two weeks later with rewrites.[8]

This approach consistently draws the actors as well as the director into the process of rewriting the play, a significant change for Wilson. When Wilson worked with Richards, the playwright's interaction with the cast was limited. Although Wilson attended all rehearsals for his plays when he worked with Richards, as previously noted, it was Richards who did most of the talking with the actors.

In contrast, Dallas' rehearsals provided an environment in which the actors participated fully, speaking freely and often with Wilson. Dallas described his workplace:

> It's usually an open forum. We all sit in there. I've never ever been one of those directors who has said to the playwright, "Now don't talk to my actors. These are my actors and you have to talk through me." My feeling is that the playwright is the source. It's his vision we're trying to get up on that stage.[9]

While working with Dallas, Wilson asked the director to rehearse scenes again and again so that he could explore what he had written, to see it anew. He found that questions from the actors about their characters helped him understand what was missing from the text. This interaction was not without its own pressures on Wilson, however:

118

Sometimes the actor might say I need something else. They'd say, "Why am I there, why don't I just do so and so?" So I say, "good question," and I go home and think about it. And they would be waiting for rewrites and I would show up with no rewrites — one day, two days, three days, four days. And the director would say we have rewrites coming on this scene and they're all waiting. And I'm waiting too. They don't know that I'm waiting, but I'm waiting for the right time to do it.[10]

But more often, the input from the actors so inspired Wilson that he wrote new material quickly.

A year after the production of *Seven Guitars*, when Dallas was not available to direct the Pittsburgh production of *Jitney*, Wilson chose Marion Isaac McClinton, an old friend who had played the role of Fielding in the 1985 production. Wilson brought what he had learned in Chicago to Pittsburgh. He and McClinton discussed the script extensively, and Wilson made the majority of his rewriting decisions during rehearsal, with McClinton, like Dallas, supporting an open and interactive environment.

Jitney began rehearsal at the Pittsburgh Public Theater in April 1996. When Wilson attended the run-through and heard the play for the first time in eleven years, his response was panic: "The second act only read twenty-six minutes. The first act was an hour and something. I thought, my first scene in *Piano Lesson* is thirty-five minutes and this whole act is twenty-six minutes so I felt I had a lot of work to do."[11]

Length, specifically long length, is a signature of Wilson's work. Most of his plays run well over three hours. One of the reasons *Jitney* was "short" was that it lacked the long story-telling monologues that characterize Wilson's mature works. Wilson remembers it was an actor, hungry for one of his stories, who pointed out this omission.

Willis Burkes, who's playing Shealy, he comes up and he says, "Say August. They ain't gonna know this is your play." I say, "What you mean?" He say, "You ain't got no monologues in it." So I say, "OK, you'll have one tomorrow," and I wrote him his monologue about Rosie.[12]

119

In fact, Wilson eventually added seven monologues to the play, and by providing the characters with these monologues detailing lives outside the action witnessed in the play, he created people who exist beyond their roles in the play's plot. As he rewrote *Jitney* in the rehearsal room, his contact with the actors encouraged and significantly influenced his writing of the stories they told.

In the original script, Doub briefly mentions his time in the army. In his rewrite, Wilson added a monologue in which Doub describes his agonizing assignment of cleaning the battlefields. Energized by the new monologue, the actor playing Doub pushed for further definition of his character. So, with a passing reference — "just like I tell my boys"— Wilson gave him children. Satisfying the actor gives Wilson pleasure.

> The actor kept working and he said, "They know that Becker worked at the mill...I think Doub worked at the railroad," So he wanted me to include that. So I said, "OK, when you say pension why don't you say railroad pension." And that made the actor happy and gave him a whole new thing. He says "I ain't too worried, I got my railroad pension." That made him somebody. That little thing made Doub somebody. The railroad, the army, has two kids. The character prior to Pittsburgh didn't have that, he was just a guy.[13]

In some cases, Wilson drew upon the real-life experience of his cast in creating the characters. Inspiration for fielding's long tale describing his work as Billy Ekstein's tailor came from the actor playing this role: Anthony Chisholm's father made suits for Count Basie. Adding these new monologues gave *Jitney* some of the fullness Wilson felt it had lacked.

> My plays that I've written since *Jitney* have that richness of character and that's what I was trying to accomplish here. The characters were more than suggested but they weren't as full as they could be. So I was trying to flesh them out more in a way that I would have done if I was writing the play now. The more the

audience knows about the character, the better experience they will have at the play. So why not make it fuller?[14]

Four of the stories Wilson added to this heavily male-dominated drama are about women, none of whom actually appears in the play; indeed, the only female character who is integral to the action is Youngblood's woman, Rena. But, as in all of Wilson's plays, the dearth of women onstage belies their importance to the men they love. Relationships with wives and lovers are crucial aspects of Wilson's portrayal of his characters as full, rounded, complicated human beings.

Wilson's ear for natural speech has grown remarkably sophisticated since he first wrote *Jitney*. His more recent characters are readily identifiable to the audience through the specific quality of their discourse, the pulse of their exchanges, and the exact selection of their words. Listening to his early work in rehearsal pushed Wilson to include many new, short exchanges between characters that reflected what he had learned about using dialogue to define and establish character as well as to create the extraordinary rhythm now a hallmark of Wilson's scripts.

But not all of Wilson's changes were additions. As he reworked *Jitney*, he found that his early, less mature efforts to clarify his story undermined his characterization. For example, on his return to the script, Wilson eliminated much of the repetitive dialogue he had included for fear that the audience would miss an important development.[15]

Wilson also captured the rhythm of his characters' speech by eliminating unnecessary stopgaps, such as overuse of one character's name by another. And he cut distracting interruptions originally written so that every character's line was in direct response to another character's questions. These and other changes reveal a shift of focus from ensuring that the story is understood to guaranteeing that the characters are true. Cumulatively, they result in a far clearer definition of the people in the play.

Overall, Wilson's presentation of his complex characters is more efficient. He now trusts that the audience will recognize certain traits without extensive repetition. Thus, for example, on his return to *Jitney*, Wilson cut many of Turnbo's negative outbursts

121

about the lives of the other drivers, readily admitting his earlier weakness: "I added too many things, really pushing it. You know, you got a good thing going and you go, oh, let me drive this into the ground. I've learned not to do that."[16]

Other cuts made in the rewrite include Doub's response to Becker's death—"It's tragic it had to happen the way it did"[17]—and the unnecessary melodrama of Youngblood's shock at hearing the news of Becker's death.[18] Instead, a more subtle Wilson allows the audience to recognize the tragedy without the signposts.

Wilson also learned to trust the actors, and his direct contact with them in rehearsal led to other kinds of changes as well. In the first draft of the script, Wilson offered frequent notes to the actors regarding their performances — "incredulous," "exasperated," "defensively," "desperate"—notes which were his way of ensuring the dialogue was spoken as Wilson heard it in his head. In the latest draft, these indicators are gone, as is the underlining Wilson had provided for the actors to indicate his preference for emphasis. Ultimately, the changes result from Wilson's confidence—confidence that more sophisticated dialogue will help the actors make appropriate acting choices, confidence that the drama created within the scene will evoke the desired response from the audience.

Wilson's more honest and developed portrayal of his characters is marked by a delicate combination of tears and laughter, and an ability to successfully blend tragedy and comedy, to show how the humor of everyday life makes its way into even the most somber moments. The later drafts of *Jitney* are funnier than the earlier ones. For example, Scene Two opens with Turnbo's admiring a centerfold. In the first draft he says to Becker, "Boy, what a man wouldn't do with that." But in later versions, Wilson allows him to continue: "Boy, what a man wouldn't do with that. If I get to heaven and she ain't there, I'm going to ask God to send me straight to hell."[19]

For the actors, working on *Jitney* was an exciting ride because of the constant changes. Wilson made some of the smaller script revisions—changes in words or occasional new lines—while the actors were rehearsing. The rest he made overnight and delivered early the next morning to McClinton, who was surprised at how well Wilson worked under pressure.

Everything he brought in fit immediately, fit right into the actors' mouths and bodies, and with what was already there. It was fascinating that the work he did on *Jitney* came out so polished and, well, correct with the time he had and the way his focus was being split at that time; he had *Seven Guitars* in New York, and a big speech coming up, and the season awards. [20]

However, despite his commitment to his new process of working intensively during rehearsal, Wilson's busy schedule kept him from nearly half of the rehearsals in Pittsburgh. As a result, even though he made significant revisions to the script there, Wilson felt that his work was still incomplete. But he did nothing more to the play until it went into rehearsal with Walter Dallas at the Crossroads Theatre in New Brunswick, almost nine months later. At that time, Wilson resumed the task of intensive revision. Wilson had chosen to bring Dallas on board because he felt that the relationship they had developed during rehearsals for *Seven Guitars* had been particularly productive and would be equally helpful to the work he needed to do on *Jitney*.

Wilson and Dallas' first discussions focused on an issue that Wilson continued to find problematic— development of the central character, Becker. The relationship between Becker and his son Booster, which stands at the core of the play, was one-dimensional. Booster's release from prison is the structural centerpiece of the play; the first act builds to it, the second act should reverberate from it. But in the early draft of the script, it was an event which had virtually no effect on either character. And so, step-by-step, beginning with the changes he made in Pittsburgh, Wilson further defined these men as individuals, and as father and son.

Booster had gone to jail for killing a woman in revenge for an unfounded accusation of rape. His sentence was death by electrocution, later commuted to life imprisonment. Becker deeply resents Booster and sees him as a murderer twice over, holding him responsible for the loss of his wife who died shortly after Booster was sentenced. He still feels devastated by the crushing of all the dreams he once held for his son.

In the first version of *Jitney*, the sketchy characterizations of Becker and Booster did not allow the potential drama of their relationship to emerge. In fact, the two men appeared together in only one scene, which followed Booster's release from the penitentiary. In that scene, they clash immediately as old arguments resurface, and Booster blasts his father for accepting what life doled out without a fight:

> What is you? You a big man? You a deacon at the church? Boss of the jitney station. A man with a responsibility. You work thirty years in the mill and ain't got a union card. Why? Because you got to work six months straight to get one. They work you five and a half months and lay you off for two weeks. Then you got to start all over. Did you ever tell them bastards to go to hell? Did you ever knock the foreman on his ass when he said you were laid off?... You accepted whatever kind of shit they threw your way. And now you want to hold that up as some kind of example for me...[21]

Becker blasts back:

> ...You want to come in here and ridicule me? "Why didn't you knock the foreman on his ass?" You wanna know why? I'll tell you why. Because I had your black ass at home crying to be fed. Crying to have a roof over your head. To have clothes to wear to school and lunch money in your pocket. That's why! Because I had a family.[22]

Their battle heats up to the point where Becker finally rejects Booster entirely: "You is my son. I birthed you into this world. But from this moment on, I'm calling the deal off. You ain't nothing to me, boy. You just another nigger on the street."[23] After that, in the original version of *Jitney*, the two men have no further contact; they remain estranged and separate.

Later in the first script, when Youngblood tells Becker that his son came by to see him, Becker responds with "If he comes back,

tell him I said to stay away from me."[24] Then, when Booster learns
of his father's death shortly afterwards, he is overcome, and in the
last scene of the play, following the funeral, Booster listens to the
drivers' praise of his father and announces that he "never knowed
him too much...but [he's] proud to be Becker's boy."[25] In the
absence of greater development, the words are flat and the emo-
tion trite.

During rehearsals in Pittsburgh, as part of his effort to deep-
en the characterizations, Wilson added an encounter in which
Booster, refusing to accept Becker's rejection, returns to the jitney
station to tell his father of his pain at their estrangement while he
was in jail. The scene shows another side of Booster; he needs his
father's approval:

> I waited for you to come to see me. I wanted to know that you
> understood that I was just trying to be the kind of man you want-
> ed me to be. That I wouldn't let nobody mess over me. I didn't
> wait but a month. Then I knew you wasn't never gonna come. I
> told myself there wasn't nothing I could do about that.[26]

Booster then tries to explain how he coped, but stops speaking as
his father, unable to respond, gathers his things and walks out,
effectively abandoning his son yet again.

For the Pittsburgh production, Wilson had made additional
script changes intended to further illuminate the Becker/Booster
relationship. Becker's inability to acknowledge his own contribution to the breach between himself and his son gains poignancy as
Wilson revealed Becker's potential as a father through his relationship with Youngblood. The young jitney driver has had a
checkered past, running the streets and fathering an illegitimate
child. By nature, Youngblood is not unlike Booster; both are
brash, hotheaded, and very much motivated by a personal sense of
justice. Indeed, when Youngblood first hears the story of
Booster's crime of shooting the girl who falsely accused him of
rape, Youngblood responds with "Served the bitch right."[27]

But with each new draft, Wilson revealed more of
Youngblood's efforts to turn his life around, action at least partly

attributable to the parental interest and encouragement he receives from Becker:

> So you bought a house, huh? Ain't nothing like owning some property. They might even call you for jury duty. Most young men be on the other side of the law. How old's the baby now?...Ain't nothing left to do now but get married.[28]

Wilson's revisions created a Youngblood who, in contrast to Booster, shows greater respect for authority, doesn't swear and has a clear life plan. He also becomes a more gentle parent; in the first draft, he asks about his child: "Where's the kid?" In later scripts he asks: "Where's my boy?"[29]

Although Becker thinks he has found in Youngblood what he has lost with his own son, Wilson wanted to show that it is Booster who has the most profound effect on Becker's behavior. So he tried, in this first revision, to reveal how Booster's return and the accompanying dredging up of the past defeat Becker.

During the Pittsburgh production, Wilson emphasized Becker's feelings of hopelessness by significantly increasing the amount of time he has kept secret from the drivers the approaching demolition of the jitney station. Doub reprimands Becker for that delay:

> It ain't like that's a small piece of news. I got rent to pay. Doctor bills. Every man in here depending on this station for their livelihood. The city's gonna board it up...you've known for two weeks...and you ain't bothered to get around to telling nobody.[30]

Becker's answer shows the depth of his defeat:

> You look up one day and all you got left is what you ain't spent. Everyday cost you something and you don't all the time realize it. I used to question God about everything. Why he harden Pharaoh's heart? Why he let Jacob steal his brother's birthright? After Ruth died I told myself I wasn't gonna ask no

more questions. Cause the answers didn't matter. They didn't
matter right then. I thought that would change but it never did.
It still don't matter after all these years.[31]

The cumulative effect of these changes was to show how destructive Becker and Booster are to one another. But when the show
closed in Pittsburgh, Wilson was dissatisfied with this picture
because it diminished any sense of what was lost with Becker's
death. Wilson wanted to make the death "bigger," more tragic in
its denial of some potential. Ultimately, he understood that if the
audience was to care about that death, it needed to feel a sense of
what could have been, and to understand that, not just through
Becker's surrogate relationship with Youngblood, but through the
give-and-take of father and son.

It was during rehearsals for the Crossroads Theatre production that Wilson tackled this problem. He was encouraged by
Walter Dallas, who agreed that the dramatic potential of the
father/son relationship had not been fully exploited:

I wasn't quite sure why we should care that Becker dies. It
seemed in the early version that I read, it seemed that we heard
people say things about Becker—he's always looking out for
other people, always taking care of things, but I didn't see him
do those things in the play.[32]

So as the actors played out the action in rehearsal, Wilson gradu-
ally concluded that the way to remedy this situation was to show a
change in Becker, one that owes something to his encounter with
Booster. In the first two drafts of *Jitney*, Becker's despair over
Booster ultimately overcomes any instinct he has to save the jitney station. In the later drafts, Becker adopts some of Booster's
defiance as his own.

To reveal the new Becker, Wilson added a scene late in the
play—the first time we see Becker after he walked out as Booster
reproached him for never visiting him in jail. In this scene, Becker
has called a meeting of the drivers to discuss how they can fight
the closing of the station. For Wilson, Becker's decision to fight,

to lead the men, and to increase their self-respect reflects a significant change in the character: "For the first time in his life, he's not just going to take what's given, what's presented to him; he's going to stand up."[33] Having heard Booster's challenge, Becker reevaluates his life choices:

> When I first come along I tried to do everything right. I figured that was the best thing to do. Even when it didn't look like they was playing fair I told myself they would come around. Time it look like you got a little something going for you, they would change the rules. Now you got to do something else. I told myself that's alright, my boy's coming. He's gonna straighten it out. I put it on somebody else. It took it off of me and put it on somebody else. I told myself as long as I could do that then I could just keep going along and making excuses for everybody. But I'm through making excuses for anybody... including myself. I ain't gonna pass it on. I say we stay here.[34]

Becker also has new lines at the end of the scene that make a clear statement about his hope for a reconciliation with his son: "Say Doub...my boy been around here? You seen him?"[35]

As Wilson moved toward revealing a bond between father and son that neither could ultimately deny, he justified what is probably the most significant change from the original script—the addition of two words as the new closing line for the play. Following Becker's funeral, all of the drivers return to the jitney station. Booster joins them briefly. Then, as he turns to leave, the phone begins to ring. A moment passes and then Booster picks up the receiver and says "Car Service." The son has come full circle, into his father's shoes, thus offering closure for the audience by providing the reconciliation Becker's death otherwise denies.[36]

Wilson believes *Jitney* appeals more to audiences than any of his other plays. He bases his belief on handshakes:

> I notice a difference when people come up and say, "Oh, I liked your play," and when people talk to you about it. With this play they grab my hand, grab both my hands and squeeze them and

128

say "Oh, I really liked it." It's that kind of thing. And I've gotten more of that with this play than almost any play.[37]

Jitney broke all box office records at the twenty-two-year-old
Pittsburgh Public Theater and also sold out its run at the
Crossroads. Its appeal is easy to define: *Jitney* is a realistic play; it
is the most contemporary in the Wilson canon; and it is the short-
est of Wilson's plays—despite its growth from 90 to 135 minutes.
It is also very funny.

The press response, however, was mixed. Praised for being "as
powerful and incisive as Wilson's others, but far funnier, and
yes, entertaining," the play was also roundly criticized for its
structure.[38]

> ...the play is unevenly plotted and overly melodramatic. All in
> all, it's a minor work in the Wilson canon. The play's center-
> piece, the story of the bitter reunion of the station manager,
> Becker and his ex-convict son, Booster, also happens to be its
> least compelling element...The play...at present feels less
> like a collection of neatly woven tales than one of loose
> strings.[39]

Disappointed but undaunted, Wilson says he will continue his
process of revising the play, production after production.
"Opening night is not the end; it's just the beginning. I'll see the
play and make notes and I know I'll continue to work on it."[40]

Jitney is scheduled for production at the Goodman Theatre,
perhaps to be followed by a run at the Manhattan Theatre Club
in New York City. As Wilson waited until the show was in
rehearsal in New Jersey to make the changes he had envisioned
in Pittsburgh, so too will he wait until the show is in rehearsal in
Chicago before he makes further changes to the script. But as
director Walter Dallas notes, the agenda is already set, and the
work will continue in the direction of strengthening the characters and their relationship to each other.

> We talked about the idea that maybe Booster needed to learn
> more about his father. He says at the end, "I didn't get to know

him the way you guys did." Well, we know that they know him because we see them working and we hear that they have a twelve- or eighteen-year history with him. But Doub, for example, never tells a story about Becker even though he's worked with the man for twelve years, been involved with the man. But he never shares anything with Booster about him. Or Fielding, who is really the one that Booster has a relationship with of the jitney drivers, says, "Yeah I knew your father when he was working at the mill. That's when I was younger." And then it's all about Fielding, the dream. We might take the opportunity for Fielding to share something with Booster, just the two of them in the room—about his father. So things like that. Finding moments where we can make more connections to each of the different stories. We're always looking for general ways to strengthen the threads of the story that finally come together.[41]

If Wilson is asked to define what he has learned about playwriting over the years, he cannot answer in specific dramaturgical terms. And, indeed, if his new process of rewriting is any indication, his work has become even more instinctive and less defined by rules than it ever was. What seems to have been most refined is not his pen but his senses—particularly his sense of people.

Wilson is confident that the play will continue to improve and appreciates that he has come far since he wrote *Jitney*.

When I started *Jitney* I didn't know you weren't supposed to write it in ten days. I just sat down and wrote it and didn't make a big thing about it. When I go to it now I go to it as a skilled craftsman...Nineteen seventy-nine versus nineteen ninety-seven. That's almost eighteen years ago. Thank God I've improved.[42]

Wilson refers to *Jitney* as a "free play"; i.e. one he did not have to create from scratch in response to pressure to provide new work. But there is, perhaps, a greater challenge in fixing an old play than in creating a new one. While *Jitney* has grown significantly over the years, it remains to be seen if it will achieve the stature of Wilson's more recently-conceived plays.

"I Ain't Sorry for Nothin' I Done"

Conclusion

At the 1996 annual conference of the Theater Communication Group, a national association of regional theaters, August Wilson issued an urgent warning: "[Black theatre is] a target for cultural imperialists who seek to propogate their ideas about the world as the only valid ideas, and see blacks as woefully deficient not only in arts and letters but in the abundant gifts of humanity."[1] Reviewing the status of black theater, Wilson challenged black artists to reconsider where, how, and for whom their plays are produced. "It is time," he said, "we took responsiblity for our talents in our own hands."[2]

Certainly Wilson is an appropriate spokesperson for the contemporary black theater, but his increasing outspokenness on racial politics in the arts has illuminated an unusual juxtapositon between his ideoogy and his own artistic practice. Indeed, Wilson's very success has provided him with a platform from which to repudiate the theatrical route he himself has followed.

Wilson's speech was no doubt inspired by a recent vogue in North American theaters for work by black playwrights. Theaters that were once almost exclusively the domain of white playwrights now make a point of including the occasional work by black artists. The ostensible motive, beyond the inherent merit of the individ-

131

ual play, is the diversification of both art and audience, a goal much lauded in the 1980s and early 1990s. In his keynote speech at the TCG Conference, Wilson, whose own plays have been extremely popular at predominantly white theaters, attacked this vogue. He denounced the trend as devastating to the life of black theater because it means that white theaters are now siphoning off money—and audiences—that would otherwise be available to black theaters. Wilson sees the effort of white theaters to become more multicultural in their selection of plays as misguided and dangerous to the black theater community.

> Doing a black play...does not change the nature of the institution or its mission. Blacks come and go and the institution remains dedicated to its ideas of "preserving culture and promoting thought." Our visitor pass expires and we never have a permanent place to hang our hat, to develop our own ideas, and to provide our community with a sense of cultural worth and self-sufficiency. The damage this does to our present institutions and our already debilitated communities is evident and significant.[3]

Offering an alternate plan for the survival and flourishing of black culture, Wilson called for the establishment of theaters devoted to the production of black plays, and challenged black artists to support these theaters with their work. Wilson's call for separate theaters is a reiteration of W.E.B. Du Bois' exhortation that African Americans should have theater which is "by us, for us, near us, and about us."

The speech—delivered to a predominantly white audience—sparked immediate discussion throughout the national theater community. Roundtables were scheduled on stages around the country; flurries of responses were printed in leading theater journals. Wilson's long-standing critic Robert Brustein, Artistic Director of the American Repertory Theater and reviewer for *The New Republic,* wrote a heated reply. Wilson and Brustein then held a public debate in New York City's Town Hall which was covered by newspapers in most major cities. Their war of words focused not only on Wilson's revolutionary ideas for the future of black theater, but also on the inconsistencies between Wilson's politics and his own creative process.

Wilson's attack on white theaters' attempts at multiculturalism, and his implicit criticism of those minority artists who participate in such efforts, are unexpected, coming as they do from a black playwright whose success has been built with the support of so many white theaters. If Wilson believes that theaters such as the Yale Repertory Theatre, the Goodman Theatre, the Old Globe, and the Huntington should not be producing black plays, then why has he continually selected them to produce his own work? Indeed, not a single Wilson play of the last twenty years has premiered at a black theater.

Some members of the theater community found Wilson's statements not only unexpected, but, in fact, hypocritical. As black playwright Suzan-Lori Parks expressed it, "August can start by having his own acclaimed plays premiere in black theaters, instead of where they premiere now. I'm sorry, but he should examine his own house." [4]

Wilson's speech also raised questions regarding his own creative process. Central to Wilson's argument against diversification is the adverse effect white theaters have on black artists who "allow others to have authority over our cultural and spiritual products." [5] Wilson warns of tremendous danger in these circumstances:

> We are being strangled by our well-meaning friends. Money spent "diversifying" the American theater, developing black audiences for white institutions, developing ideas of color-blind casting...only strengthens and solidifies this stranglehold by making our artists subject to the paternalistic notions of white institutions that dominate and control art. [6]

Is Wilson thus admitting that in developing his plays at white institutions with primarily white audiences he, too, has endangered his creative cultural identity? When long, rambling stories are cut from his plays, when supernatural elements are pushed out of the dramatic spotlight, when conclusions with greater closure are sought, does this demonstrate the influence of the "paternalistic notions of white institutions?"

At first glance, the answer seems to be yes. All of Wilson's dramas have been strongly influenced by the American process of play development—a process in which new plays are open to significant professional and public review in the course of their creation. At institutions recognized within the American theater as bastions for the development of new work—New Dramatists, the O'Neill Playwrights Conference, the Yale Repertory Theatre, and the Goodman Theatre are only a few of the dozens in existence—Wilson's plays have been staged by eager personnel, poked by inquisitive directors and dramaturgs, molded by ambitious artistic directors, and deluged by comments from theater professionals. Despite the fact that the text of Wilson's speech makes this seem a treacherous undertaking, he has been committed to this process.

Although Wilson has never before raised this issue, his words give a new racially-oriented twist to the old debate about whether mainstream theaters, consciously or unconsciously, exert an influence which pushes playwrights into a more commercial mold. Many contemporary theater artists believe that the traditional practitioners of American dramaturgy may not truly have the playwright's individuality in mind. Playwright and dramaturg Tom St. George, who has been an active participant at the O'Neill Conference, is outspoken regarding the risks of the American process of play development.

> One of the worst side effects in dramaturgical work in general, and in new play work in American theater in particular, is that there is a real impatience with anything that isn't understood and can't be explained. It's very, very hard for a play to get through a developmental program without people wrinkling their nose at something they don't understand. And, sometimes, work gets blanded out, particularly if it's a younger writer who is anxious to please everyone. August doesn't fall into that category, but I wonder if some of that didn't happen to his work, particularly earlier on.[7]

134

Although Wilson has never spoken publicly of his own plays in this context, the possible "blanding out" of his work has been a topic of discussion for those who have worked with him or followed the progress of his work. Critic and dramaturg Michael Feingold who, as noted, has worked closely with Wilson at the O'Neill, feels that "the more traditional play innately isn't the kind of play Wilson starts out writing; he is writing something much more free in form."[8]

Some Wilson critics, as well as some who believe themselves his truest fans, argue that the pressures of the developmental institutions tend to produce plays written in the western, realistic tradition, and have moved Wilson away from his impulse to write in a mode that is closer to African literary and performance traditions, and more clearly reflective of the influence of his four "B's." Indeed, study of the progressive drafts of many of Wilson's scripts supports this argument as it reveals a consistent movement toward a more mainstream style. For example, Wilson's original ending for *The Piano Lesson,* with Boy Willie endlessly fighting off Sutter's ghost, was lost in favor of greater closure as the ghost is defeated and Boy Willie and Berniece amicably resolve their dispute over the piano.

Those who have watched the development of Wilson's plays see a clear difference between where he starts and where he ends, often finding in Wilson's first impulse an energy lacking in the more "polished" versions that ultimately get produced. Feingold states, "There's always something fascinating to me in the early drafts of his plays. And it's rarely the structure and the resolution which a Broadway producer would think of as being important in a play—you know, what happens and what's the socko ending?"[9] Gitta Honegger, Resident Dramaturg emeritus of the Yale Rep, "loved when August's plays were basically sprawling all over, because he's a poet. Before it was streamlined or whatever you want to call that, it was a mess, but it was wonderful."[10]

But Honegger recognizes the inevitability of that "streamlining" once the plays enter the system. She says the usual approach is to evaluate in terms of traditional dramaturgy. "You wonder about the options. You hear the voice a playwright has, which may be completely unusual and completely non-traditional, and then you think, "Well, what should we do with it?" [11] "We" are the directors, dramaturgs, critics, theater managers, and other artists, who work at mainstream white theaters, and who help to shape Wilson's plays.

How then is Wilson's choice to participate actively in this process to be understood in light of the arguments he has recently presented? Perhaps Wilson believed his work at the white theaters would be less compromised because he was collaborating with a black director, Lloyd Richards. But Richards' traditional dramaturgy may, in fact, have limited the scope of Wilson's work. Richards often focused on the structure of the plays, seeking to "make a dramatic event out of the material." [12] It was Richards, for example, who targeted the "problematic" split focus of the original *Ma Rainey* script, which Wilson changed to a more traditionally unified action.

But Richards' voice was not the only one Wilson heard, or the only opinion. Michael Feingold, for one, was very vocal in his disagreement:

> I disagreed with Lloyd about what would be a full and effective version of *Ma Rainey*. He wanted it to be a play in the old Broadway sense and I've never been totally convinced that it was August's destiny to write those. [13]

But, as Honegger noted, Richards was extremely influential:

> Lloyd knew very clearly what he wanted. Now myself, having worked with Lloyd over the years, pretty much I knew what he wanted or what his way of thinking was, and there was no question but that this was what's going to be done. [14]

Although Richards claims to promote fullness of expression as opposed to conventional structure, his work on Wilson's plays has been dramaturgically conservative, as described by many, including Honegger:

> Lloyd, being a long practitioner of the theater, and having had the O'Neill so many years, knows very well what the structure of

a play should be, using the model, I would say, more or less, of the well-made play, in the Aristotelian sense.[15]

Wilson himself never studied the well-made, Aristotelian-influenced play, which serves as the template for, and often the measure of, Eurocentric, western drama. According to Wilson, when he began playwriting, he had not read any dramatic theory and his contact with western-style dramatic literature was very limited. But over time, he has clearly come to understand and to apply to his own inherently non-traditional dramaturgy the principles of standard Eurocentric dramatic structure. Richards did not speak to Wilson about craft, but says, "Wilson had to learn to write dialogue and he had to begin to dramatize. Then he learned other old tricks along the way."[16] Thus, the environment may have changed not only the art but also the artist, resulting in the assimilation of an ideology rather than outright imposition.

Despite the abundance of input he has received from Richards and others, Wilson has always retained creative control of his work. But his own ideas about his work have changed in the course of his interactions with them. Indeed, those who have worked with Wilson on the development of his plays remark on how much he has internalized the pressure to write structurally traditional drama, as perhaps most clearly demonstrated by *Fences*, in which Wilson, by his own admission, set out to prove he could write a play in a conventional style. Richards says any pressure Wilson felt "he imposed upon himself, and I don't think he did that badly."[17] Indeed, *Fences* is Wilson's most commercially successful play. Thus if Wilson was indeed "subject to paternalistic notions," herein defined as pressure to write within the traditional western style, the conflict was not as clear-cut as Wilson described in his speech. And its resolution was perhaps bred from Wilson's contention that he was able to strike a balance.

Wilson knows he straddles two worlds, but believes himself to be integrating two traditions, and in so doing, paying homage to both:

In one guise, the ground I stand on has been pioneered by the Greek dramatists — by Euripides, Aeschylus, and Sophocles —

by William Shakespeare, by Shaw and Ibsen, and by the American dramatists Eugene O'Neill, Arthur Miller, and Tennessee Williams. In another guise, the ground that I stand on has been pioneered by my grandfather, by Nat Turner, by Denmark Vesey, by Martin Delaney, Marcus Garvey, and the Honorable Elijah Muhammad.[18]

But Michael Feingold believes successive drafts of Wilson's plays reveal a process not so much of integration as of subtraction — the displacing of one aesthetic in favor of another.

I think one thing you get in August is two very different aesthetics going on. He has conflicted impulses. He wants to do two quite different things at the same time.

One is a sort of condition of talk, as music, that makes the plays conversation pieces which are sometimes very static and very beautiful. And the other one is an effort to do a well-crafted play in the old style.

I think if you look at what he writes before it gets to the O'Neill, it's more of a static conversation piece. Then, in the process of the O'Neill, and definitely at Yale, he moves it toward the well-made play.[19]

Still, non-traditional elements such as supernatural events and extensive monologues, contained in the original drafts which continued to reflect Wilson's dramatic instincts, were maintained in later versions. Thus, Wilson believes he successfully integrated and reconciled diverse impulses. Others disagree, some quite publicly. Gerald Bordman writes in *The Oxford Companion to American Theater*: "This profusion of awards [for Wilson's work] is baffling....his plays are an unhomogenized melange of styles and techniques."[20]

Ironically, even those who agree that Wilson has successfully incorporated a more familiar and thus universally "acceptable"

138

structure advance an argument that inadvertenly validates Wilson's political point. *The Cambridge Guide to Theater* includes this reference: "... Wilson has certainly emerged as the richest theatrical voice in the United States of the past decade and has managed to transcend the categorization of black playwright through his dissection of black families and communities to a broad-based audience."[21] The implicit assumption here is that a black playwright must abandon a unique cultural identity in order to reach a wide audience, precisely the point that Wilson was making when he warned of white theatrical co-optation of the black experience.

If there is some truth to such an assumption, then the issue Wilson raised in his speech is a serious one: Can a black playwright working in the mainstream white theater retain a cultural identity? Wilson acknowledges that the theater in which he has chosen to work has its foundation in the "European theater," yet says he "reserves the right to amend, to explore, to add our African consciousness and our African aesthetic to the art we produce."[22] If this right can truly be reserved, as Wilson espouses, then the danger for a black writer working at a white theater may not, ultimately, be as destructive as Wilson himself argues. But reserving the right, exercising it partially, and exercising it fully are different things. And to exercise it fully may be to alienate much of the audience, not to mention the Pulitzer committee and white theaters in general.

Certainly, Wilson's current artistic stature mitigates that danger for him and has likely inspired recent professional choices that initially indicate a reshaping of his work in accordance with his own internal mandates. For example, his latest plays do not reflect the influence of traditional western dramaturgy as strongly as his previous plays do; *Two Trains Running, Seven Guitars,* and the revised *Jitney,* for example, do not have the easily identified rising action of *Ma Rainey* or *Fences.* The structures of all of these later plays indicate a move to recapture the style of the first drafts of previous plays, including, for example, more storytelling and less cause-and-effect-driven plot. But these new directions may be destined for short life, undermined by Wilson's history, his relationships, and his personal ambitious goals.

None of the recent plays embodying this alternative aesthetic received the critical acclaim of those which immediately preceded them (*Ma Rainey, Fences, Joe Turner*, and *Piano Lesson*), and Wilson was unhappy with the duration of the runs and the public response. Voices which were usually supportive joined those from whom Wilson was used to hearing criticism to express their disapproval. Henry Louis Gates Jr., Chairman of the Afro-American Studies Department at Harvard University and a Wilson enthusiast, wrote in *The New Yorker* that "an unruly luxuriance of language — an ability to ease between trash talk and near-choral transport — is Wilson's great gift; sometimes you wish he were less generous with that gift, for it can come at the expense of conventional dramaturgic virtues like pacing and the sense of closure." [23] Critic Robert Brustein said of *Seven Guitars*, "However colorful its subject matter, it cannot ramble willy-nilly for two and a half hours before establishing a line of action." [24]

Perhaps these and other similar responses have played some role in Wilson's recent critique of contemporary criticism. In the past, Wilson has spoken of the value he places on criticism as a tool to sharpen his drama.

> I respect the critic's point of view. Now, I don't necessarily make changes in the play because I read one review or another. But I take everything very seriously. And if a person says a certain thing, then I go back and look at the script and try to see why they said what they said. Then I decide if I'm going to make a change. [25]

Wilson himself has acknowledged the impact of criticism, admitting its role in determining, for example, his creative approach to *Fences*, which, as noted earlier, was written partially in response to the white reviewers who had criticized *Ma Rainey* for its bifurcated focus.

But the mixed reviews of his own more recent work and work by other African-American playwrights has perhaps sparked Wilson's reconsideration of the role of the critic. In his keynote speech, Wilson called upon professional critics to bring a broader perspective to their work.

All theatergoers have opinions about the work they witness. Critics have an informed opinion. Sometimes it may be necessary for them to gather more information to become more informed. As playwrights grow and develop, as the theater changes, the critic has an important responsibility to guide and encourage that growth. However, in the discharge of their duties, it may be necessary for them to also grow and develop. A stagnant body of critics, operating from the critical criteria of forty years ago, makes for a stagnant theater without the fresh and abiding influence of contemporary ideas.

A critic who can recognize a German neo-romantic influence should also be able to recognize an American influence from blues or black church rituals, or any other contemporary American influence.[26]

Thus, on the one hand, Wilson craves criticism from minds which have "gathered more information," which can meet him halfway as he "amends and explores." But, at the same time, he knows that the cost of the kind of success he has had is that he cannot legitimately advocate evaluative criteria derived from outside western traditions.

We do not ask, we do not seek, nor do we want special treatment. Inasmuch as we are part of western theater, work should be judged on those terms and principles as outlined by Aristotle in his *Poetics*. We have never asked to stand outside of that or to have our work treated differently or judged by different standards or criteria because we are black.[27]

And, given his awareness of the importance of the critics to the survival of the theaters in which he has chosen to work, and his recognition, and ultimately acceptance, that his work will be judged according to the criteria of traditional European dramaturgy, it is difficult to understand how he can both "amend and explore" and expect to continue, to enjoy the commercial success he has had to date at white theaters.

In the Town Hall debate, Robert Brustein challenged Wilson to bring his work to black theaters. In what seemed to his supporters a glaring omission, Wilson did not then mention his upcoming production of *Jitney*. At that time, *Jitney* had already been scheduled for spring 1997 production at the Crossroads Theater, in New Brunswick, N.J., described by its Artistic Director, Ricardo Khan, as "a professional environment for artists in black theater to develop, explore and practice their craft."[28]

The decision to produce at the Crossroads was Wilson's idea. But perhaps he did not feel comfortable invoking it in his self-defense, since it was an idea primarily driven by a change in the production schedule at the Huntington Theater in Boston, which would have left the *Jitney* production idle for a full year after its run in Pittsburgh. In fact, Wilson has stated that his decision to have *Jitney* produced at Crossroads was not a political one.

> It was not a consideration. It just was a theater that might do the play and it seemed like a good idea. I wasn't totally unaware that they were a black theater. But I didn't say, "Oh, let me go and seek out a black theater." It's just that there we were talking last July or August 1996, and we were talking about going into rehearsal in Boston in September 1997 and it seemed like such a long time away. I thought "Can't we do it before then?" And there was the chance to do it at Crossroads.[29]

Indeed, despite his awareness of Crossroads as the only organization within the League of Regional Theaters (LORT) which consistently produces work by African-American playwrights, Wilson had not considered them for production of any of his previous plays. He explains that he did not know much about the theater and that it was his recent social contact with Khan that encouraged him to bring *Jitney* to Crossroads. Khan welcomed the opportunity both because of his long-standing artistic respect for Wilson and because black theaters need the press, prestige, and box office income that a Wilson play can offer.

Wilson admits to finding a greater sense of "community" at Crossroads than at other theaters in which he has worked, and he was impressed with the dedication of its artists and staff. But by his own admission, Wilson's next play is more likely to premiere at one of those "white theaters" that offer higher production values. It is a catch-22; without money, small black theaters cannot raise their levels of production sufficiently to attract an August Wilson; without an August Wilson, they cannot attract the money. So, despite a foray to the Crossroads, Wilson will continue his former associations, acknowledging that he has "very carefully worked out a relationship with various theaters that have supported my work."[30] Support began with an open door for a little-known playwright; support continues with high-quality productions, expansive audiences, and a ready road to Broadway—opportunities few, if any, black theaters can offer.

Still, Wilson is personally addressing the issues he raised in his speech. In spite of his relative comfort at those "various theaters," during his most recent productions at the Goodman Theatre and the Pittsburgh Public Theater, Wilson altered his method of revising his plays in a way that seems intended to ensure the integrity of his work. He is now doing most of his revisions as an organic part of the rehearsal process which means that he can both open himself to input from the many black theater artists with whom he works and, at the same time, free himself from the kind of external pressure that his former process entailed. Previously, he did most of his rewriting immediately following a production, so that it was more likely to have been influenced both by the public and by the critical response to the play. Now that the bulk of his revisions are done during rehearsals, Wilson does not redraft his plays immediately after they open and get reviewed. Rather, he waits until the play begins rehearsals for its next production. In the case of *Jitney*, that was almost a full year. Thus, Wilson has a longer period of time to filter or maybe to forget the public and critical response. Still, if Wilson's plays continue to follow the route to which he has become accustomed, he knows his next venue will be a large regional theater within the white establishment, financially dependent on strong box office, and tuned into word from the critics.

Ultimately, it will be up to Wilson to decide whether the style, structure, and content of his plays are affected by the imperative to fill such theaters which require audiences large enough that they will of necessity be multiracial. Will that mean, as he himself said it did in his speech, that he must then make a choice between art "that is conceived and designed to entertain white society and art that feeds the spirit and celebrate the life of black Americans by designing its strategies for survival and prosperity?"[31] Again, Wilson's words and deeds clash.

Although Wilson's speech seems to deny the possibility that any playwright who seeks a white audience can simultaneously speak powerfully to a black audience, his own plays suggest otherwise. And he seems almost willfully blind to the reasons his work might appeal to a white audience. Explaining his popularity with white audiences in sociological terms, Wilson says:

> The rush is on to do anything that's black. Largely through my plays, what the theaters have found out is that they had this white audience that was starving to get a little understanding of what was happening with the black population, because they very seldom come into contact with them so they're curious. The white theaters have discovered that there is a market for that.[32]

But it is doubtful that the white audience response to Wilson's plays is merely enthusiastic voyeurism, issuing from "curiosity" about a remote people. And it is unlikely that this is all Wilson intends. Certainly Wilson creates plays which "feed the spirit and celebrate the life of black Americans." His plays are a vital encapsulation of African-American history and contemporary life. They are quests for historical and spiritual truths, and they are very specific to the African-American experience. But Wilson himself recognizes that "being a black artist does not mean that you have to disengage yourself from the world, and your concerns as a global citizen or from the ideas of love, honor, duty, betrayal, etc., that are the concerns of all great art."[33]

White audiences attend Wilson's plays precisely because he has not disengaged himself from universal concerns and ideas. He may claim, in the course of arguing for separate theaters, that "we can meet on the common ground of theater...but we cannot meet on the common ground of experience,"[34] but racially diverse audiences come to Wilson's plays because he has succeeded in creating powerful dramas recognizable to all who encounter them; they come because he can simultaneously feed both the black and white spirit. Black audiences will continue to support Wilson regardless of where his work is produced. And, in spite of his call for separatism, white theaters and their predominantly white audiences will continue to support Wilson as well. As expressed by critic Michael Scassera, "Wilson need not consider his work universal for it to be so."[35]

The early drafts of all of Wilson's plays—heard for the first time at New Dramatists or the O'Neill Playwrights Conference or The Yale Rep or The Goodman Theatre—were powerful and moving. Many plays by other playwrights begin and end their theatrical lives with no further work done on them. But over months and years, Wilson revises, experiments, focuses, redefines, in response to opinions from many conflicting voices. The result—dramatic texts very close to the original vision in the strength, energy, and depth of their message, and yet very far in style and commercial viability—speak to the influence of the American play development system, for better or for worse.

Wilson has consistently received powerful input from artists whose tendency was to push the playwright to include traditional elements of western drama. And Wilson understands that this input, about which he warns other black theater artists in his keynote address, is the same input which has helped transform his work into drama that has found large, enthusiastic audiences. Indeed, it is unlikely that a young writer who follows Wilson's words and not his deeds, will achieve his prominence.

Whether directors, dramaturgs, critics, audience members, or actors have in any way limited Wilson's work, the collaborative process in which he has participated has resulted in great critical and commercial success for him. It is difficult to dismiss pressure that is rewarded with tremendous audience response, as well as two Pulitzer Prizes. Wilson himself expresses no regrets. Reviewing his work, he claims, "I ain't sorry for nothin' I done."[36]

Thus Wilson has come to terms with the existing American

theater and learned to work within it. But he has not done so without question—not without raising issues about its foundations and not without calling for change. If, indeed, success in the contemporary theater in any way mandates the moderation of an individual voice, then the process through which plays come to production on our stages needs to be reformed. The issues of loss of cultural identity are profound, and despite a certain discordance between what he says and what he does, Wilson is a worthy leader of "a movement to reignite and reunite our people's positive energy for a political and social change."[37]

Notes

Notes

The Process of Playwriting

1. August Wilson quoted in Aubrey Hampton, "August Wilson, Playwright," *Organica*, Summer 1988, p. 24.

2. Alain Locke and W.E.B. Du Bois quoted in Sandra Shannon, *The Dramatic Vision of August Wilson* (Howard University Press, Washington, D.C., 1995), p. 23.

3. August Wilson quoted in Myron Schwartzman, *Romare Bearden: His Life and Art* (New York: Harry Abrams, Inc., 1990), p. 8.

4. August Wilson, interview conducted by the author, February 1994.

5. The real name of the historical figure was changed as he was immortalized in blues music and Joe Turney became Joe Turner.

6. Wilson interview.

7. Ibid.

8. Charles Dutton, interview conducted by the author, December 1993.

9. Roscoe Lee Browne quoted in Jerry Tallmer, "Hearing Voices," *Playbill* for *Two Trains Running*, April 1991, pp. 11-12.

10. August Wilson, "August Wilson Responds," *American Theatre*, October 1996, p. 106.

11. August Wilson, "The Ground on Which I Stand," Wilson's keynote address of June 26 to the Theatre Communications Group National Conference, reprinted in *American Theatre*, September 1996, p. 73.

August Arrives

1. August Wilson, interview conducted by the author, February 1994.

2. August Wilson, interview conducted by the author, April 1997.

3. Ibid.

4. Wilson interview, 1994.

5. Wilson interview, 1997.

6. Ibid.

7. Ibid.

8. New Dramatists. *New Dramatists Fact Sheet* (New York: New Dramatists, 1994).

9. Wilson interview, 1997.

10. Wilson interview, 1994.

11. He was preceded by Eugene O'Neill, Robert Sherwood, George S. Kaufman, Tennessee Williams, and Edward Albee.

12. Wilson interview, 1994.

13. August Wilson quoted in Mervyn Rothstein, "Round Five for a Theatrical Heavyweight," *The New York Times*, 15 April, 1990, Arts & Leisure Section, p. 1.

14. August Wilson, "I Want a Black Director," in *May All Your Fences Have Gates:: Essays on the Drama of August Wilson*, ed. Alan Nadell (Iowa City: University of Iowa Press, 1994), p. 200.

The Four "B's"

1. August Wilson, *Fences* (New York: Plume Books, 1987), pp. 78-9. In discussing his own work, Wilson would later change nothing to nothin'.

2. August Wilson quoted in Myron Schwartzman, *Romare Bearden: His Life and Art* (New York: Harry Abrams, Inc., 1990), p. 8.

3. August Wilson, interview conducted by the author, February 1994.

4. August Wilson, *The Piano Lesson* (New York: Penguin Books, 1990), p. 108.

5. Wilson interview.

6. August Wilson quoted in Don Nelson, "August Arrives," *Daily News*, 6 March, 1988, p. 5.

7. August Wilson, *Joe Turner's Come and Gone* (New York: Plume Books, 1988), p. 51.

8. Romare Bearden quoted in Calvin Tomkins, "Putting Something Over Something Else," *The New Yorker*, 28 November, 1977, p. 60.

9. August Wilson, *Two Trains Running* (New York: Penguin Books, 1993), p. 31. The title of the play, however, comes from the blues song which includes the lines "two trains running, neither going my way."

10. August Wilson quoted in Hedy Weiss, "A Playwright Pays Homage to a Painter,"*Chicago Sun Times*, 22 September, 1991, Section E, p.7.

11. Wilson interview.

12. August Wilson, dedication to *The Homecoming* (unpublished property of August Wilson).

13. Wilson, *The Homecoming*, pp.14-16.

14. Ibid., p. 17.

15. August Wilson, *Ma Rainey's Black Bottom*, published version (New York: New American Library, 1985), n.pag.

16. Ibid., p.79.

17. Ibid., p. 71.

18. Ibid., p. 60.

19. August Wilson, *Seven Guitars* (unpublished property of August Wilson, 1995).

20. Wilson, *The Piano Lesson*, p. 101.

21. Wilson, *Joe Turner's Come and Gone*, p. 67. As the song evolved, Turney became Turner.

22. Wilson, *The Piano Lesson*, pp. 39-40.

23. Wilson interview.

24. Amiri Baraka quoted in Larry Neal, *Visions of a Liberated Future: Black Arts Movement Writings* (New York: Thunder's Mouth Press, 1989), p. x.

25. Wilson interview.

26. LeRoi Jones, *Home: Social Essays* (New York: William Morrow and Co., 1966), p. 210-11.

27. Wilson, *The Homecoming*, p. 8.

28. LeRoi Jones, *Dutchman and The Slave* (New York: William Morrow and Co., 1964), p. 34.

29. Wilson interview.

30. Ibid.

31. August Wilson, *Ma Rainey's Black Bottom*, version II (unpublished property of August Wilson, 1982), p. 36.

32. August Wilson, *Fences*, version II (unpublished property of The Eugene O'Neill Theater Center, 1983), p. 8.

33. Wilson interview.

34. Wilson, *Ma Rainey's Black Bottom*, published version, p. 98.

35. Wilson, *Joe Turner's Come and Gone*, p. 92.

36. Ibid., p. 93.

37. Ibid., p. 15.

38. Wilson, *Ma Rainey's Black Bottom*, published version, p. 17.

39. Ibid., p. 79.

40. Wilson, *Joe Turner's Come and Gone*, pp. 53-4.

41. Wilson interview.

42. Wilson, *The Piano Lesson*, p. 106.

43. Wilson interview.

The Consequence of Tolerance

1. August Wilson, interview conducted by the author, February 1994.

2. Lloyd Richards quoted in Chip Brown, "The Light in August," *Esquire*, April 1989, p. 125.

3. August Wilson, *Ma Rainey's Black Bottom*, published version (New York: New American Library, 1985), p. 82.

4. Ibid.

5. Ibid., pp. 33, 75, 84, 85.

6. Ibid., p. 80.

7. August Wilson, *Ma Rainey's Black Bottom*, version II (unpublished property of the Eugene O'Neill Theater Center, July 1982), p. 51.

8. Wilson, *Ma Rainey's Black Bottom*, published version, p. 94.

9. Ibid., p. 79.

10. Wilson, *Ma Rainey's Black Bottom*, version III (unpublished property of August Wilson, August 1982), p. 66.

11. Wilson, *Ma Rainey's Black Bottom*, published version, p. 107.

12. Ibid., p. 108.

13. Wilson, *Ma Rainey's Black Bottom*, version II, p. 60.

14. Wilson, *Ma Rainey's Black Bottom*, published version, p. 109.

15. Wilson, *Ma Rainey's Black Bottom*, version IV (unpublished property of the Yale Repertory Theatre, January 1984), p. I:9.

16. Ibid., p. I:30.

17. Wilson, *Ma Rainey's Black Bottom*, published version, p. 39.

18. Ibid., p. 71.

The Problematic Practice

1. *Program for the 1997 National Playwrights Conference* (New York: Playbill, 1997), p. 11.

2. August Wilson, interview conducted by the author, February 1994.

3. Wilson was surprised to find that most people didn't approve of the change and remembers it was probably three-to-one in favor of the old title.

4. August Wilson quoted in Mel Gussow, "Fine Tuning The Piano Lesson," *New York Times Magazine*, 10 September, 1989, p. 18.

5. William Partlan, interview conducted by the author, November 1993.

6. Ibid.

7. Amy Salz, interview conducted by the author, November 1993.

8. Ibid.

9. Partlan interview.

10. Ibid.

11. Ibid.

12. Ibid. Frank Rich was the drama critic for *The New York Times*.

13. Wilson interview.

14. Ibid.

15. Ibid.

16. Ibid.

17. Michael Feingold, interview conducted by the author, January 1994.

18. Wilson interview.

19. Salz interview.

20. Ibid.

21. Ibid.

22. Ibid.

23. Feingold interview.

24. Kirk Aanes, interview conducted by the author, January 1994.

25. Salz interview.

The Complexity of Conflict

1. August Wilson, interview conducted by the author, February 1994.

2. August Wilson, *Fences*, version I (unpublished property of August Wilson, 1982), p. 16.

3. Ibid., p. 50.

4. August Wilson, *Fences*, version III, *Theater*, Summer/Fall, 1985, p. 44.

5. Wilson, *Fences*, published version (New York: Plume Books, 1986), p. 70.

6. Wilson interview.

7. Wilson, *Fences*, published version, p. 86.

8. Wilson, *Fences*, version I, p. 28.

9. Wilson, *Fences*, published version, p. 35.

10. Wilson, *Fences*, version I, p. 86.

11. Wilson, *Fences*, published version, p. 87.

12. Ibid., p. 100.

13. Ibid., p. 70.

14. Ibid., p. 74.

15. Ibid., p. 71.

16. August Wilson, *Fences*, version II (unpublished property of the Eugene O'Neill Theater Center, August 1983), p. 69, and Wilson, *Fences*, version III, p. 59.

17. Wilson, *Fences*, version III, p. 59.

18. Wilson, *Fences*, version II, p. 42.

19. Wilson, *Fences*, published version, p. 63.

The Cultural Connection

1. August Wilson, interview conducted by the author, February 1994.

2. As mentioned earlier, by the time the song was recorded, the named had been changed from Turney into Turner.

3. August Wilson, *Joe Turner's Come and Gone*, published version (New York: Plume Books, 1988), p. 10.

4. August Wilson, *Joe Turner's Come and Gone*, version III, *Theater*, Summer/Fall, 1986, p. 77.

5. Ibid., p. 74.

6. August Wilson, *Joe Turner's Come and Gone*, version II (unpublished property of the Eugene O'Neill Theater Center, 1984), p. 28.

7. August Wilson, *Mill Hand's Lunch Bucket*, version I (unpublished property of August Wilson, 1983), p. 55.

8. Wilson, *Joe Turner's Come and Gone*, published version, p. 46.

9. Ibid., pp. 10-11.

10. Wilson, *Joe Turner's Come and Gone*, version III, p. 67.

11. Ibid.

12. Wilson, *Joe Turner's Come and Gone*, published version, p. 94.

13. Wilson, *Joe Turner's Come and Gone*, version III, p. 68.

14. Wilson, *Joe Turner's Come and Gone*, version II, p. 22.

15. Wilson, *Joe Turner's Come and Gone*, published version, p. 71.

16. Wilson, *Joe Turner's Come and Gone*, version II, p. 44-5.

17. Wilson, *Joe Turner's Come and Gone*, version II, p. 44, and Wilson, *Joe Turner's Come and Gone*, version III, p. 79.

18. Wilson, *Joe Turner's Come and Gone*, version II, p. 26.

19. Ibid., p. 25.

20. Wilson, *Joe Turner's Come and Gone*, version I, p. 26.

21. Wilson, *Joe Turner's Come and Gone*, version II, p. 26.

22. Wilson, *Joe Turner's Come and Gone*, version I, p. 27.

23. Wilson, *Joe Turner's Come and Gone*, version II, p. 61.

24. Wilson, *Joe Turner's Come and Gone*, version III, p. 85.

25. Wilson, *Joe Turner's Come and Gone*, version II, p. 62

26. Wilson, *Joe Turner's Come and Gone*, published version, p. 77.

27. Ibid., p. 10.

28. Ibid., p. 91.

29. Wilson, *Joe Turner's Come and Gone*, version II, p. 27.

30. Ibid., p. 69.

31. Wilson, *Joe Turner's Come and Gone*, published version, pp. 93-4.

32. Wilson interview.

The Final Knockout

1. August Wilson, interview conducted by the author, February 1994.

2. Lloyd Richards quoted in Richard Bernstein, "Rescuing Black Voices from the Past," *The New York Times*, 27 March, 1988, Arts & Leisure Section, p. 34.

3. Wilson interview.

4. Ibid.

5. Gitta Honegger, interview conducted by the author, January 1994.

6. August Wilson quoted in Dennis Watlington, "Hurdling Fences," *Vanity Fair*, April 1989, p. 109.

7. Lloyd Richards, interview conducted by the author, January 1994.

8. Wilson quoted in Watlington, "Hurdling Fences," p. 108.

9. Richards interview.

10. Ibid.

11. Ibid.

12. Wilson interview.

13. Honegger interview.

14. Charles Dutton, interview conducted by the author, December 1993.

15. Ibid.

16. Kim Powers, interview conducted by the author, November 1993.

17. Richards interview.

18. Richards quoted in Bernstein, "Rescuing Black Voices from the Past," p. 34.

19. Richards interview.

20. Ibid.

21. Ibid.

22. Ibid.

23. Ibid.

24. Wilson interview.

25. James Earl Jones, interview conducted by the author, November 1993.

26. Mary Alice, interview conducted by the author, January 1994.

27. Wilson interview.

28. Ibid.

29. Ms. Hayes refused this author's request for an interview.

30. Wilson interview.

31. Ibid.

32. Richards interview.

33. Lloyd Richards quoted in Mervyn Rothstein, "Round Five for a Theatrical Heavyweight," *The New York Times*, 15 April 1990, Arts & Leisure Section, p. 20.

34. Wilson interview.

35. Dutton interview.

36. Wilson interview.

37. Ibid.

38. David Moore, interview conducted by the author, October 1993.

39. Ibid.

40. Honegger interview.

41. Richards interview.

42. Richards quoted in Bernstein, "Rescuing Black Voices from the Past," p. 34.

Jitney

1. August Wilson, interview conducted by the author, April 1997.

2. Ibid.

3. Ibid.

4. Ibid.

5. Ibid.

6. Ibid.

7. Walter Dallas, interview conducted by the author, April 1997.

8. Ibid.

9. Ibid.

10. Wilson interview.

11. Ibid.

12. Ibid.

13. Ibid.

14. Ibid.

15. The following dialogue is from August Wilson, *Jitney*, version I (unpublished property of August Wilson, 1979), p. 43.
    DOUB: What...you and Turnbo had some words?
    FIELDING: Turnbo pulled a gun on him.
    DOUB: He did what!
    FIELDING: Pulled a gun on him.

16. Wilson interview.

17. Wilson, *Jitney*, version I, p. 53.

18. The following dialogue is from Wilson, *Jitney*, version I, p. 52.
    DOUB: Ain't you heard?
    YOUNGBLOOD: Heard what?
    DOUB: Becker was killed in an accident down at the mill yesterday.
    YOUNGBLOOD: Killed? Becker?

19. Wilson, *Jitney*, version II (unpublished property of August Wilson, 1996), p. 17.

20. Marion Isaac McClinton, interview conducted by the author, July 1997.

Wilson prides himself on his ability to evaluate his own writing. As McClinton remembers: "There's something he told me once: that all playwrights write badly as well as write good. The trick is to be able to recognize your own bad writing."

21. Wilson, *Jitney*, version I, p. 38.

22. Ibid., p. 39.

23. Ibid.

24. Ibid., p. 51.

25. Ibid., p. 59.

26. Wilson, *Jitney*, version II, p. 69.

27. Ibid, p. 34.

28. August Wilson, *Jitney*, version III (unpublished property of August Wilson, 1997), p. 69.

29. Wilson, *Jitney*, version I, p. 49, & Wilson, *Jitney*, version II, p. 67.

30. Wilson, *Jitney*, version II, p. 27.

31. Ibid.

32. Dallas interview.

33. Wilson interview.

34. Wilson, *Jitney*, version III, p. 72B.

35. Ibid., p. 72D.

36. As Wilson says, "Give me that old time religion, if it's good enough for my mother, it's good enough for me."

37. Wilson interview.

38. Peter Filichia, "*Jitney* Gives Audience a Joy Ride," *Newark Star Ledger*, 22 April, 1997, p. 17D.

39. Peter Marks, "Cabdriver's Melancholy Resists the Liquid Cure," *The New York Times*, 23 May, 1997, Section C, p. 3.

40. Wilson interview.

41. Dallas interview.

42. Wilson interview.

" I Ain't Sorry For Nothin' I Done"

1. August Wilson, "The Ground on Which I Stand," Wilson's keynote address of June 26, 1996 to the Theatre Communications Group National Conference, reprinted in *American Theatre*, September 1996, p. 71.

2. Ibid., p. 73.

3. August Wilson, "August Wilson Responds," *American Theatre*, October 1996, p. 105.

4. Suzan-Lori Parks quoted in Henry Louis Gates Jr., "Chitlin Circuit," *The New Yorker*, 3 February, 1997, p. 47. Ms. Parks' plays are most often produced at black theaters.

5. Wilson, "The Ground on Which I Stand," p. 72.

6. Wilson, "August Wilson Responds," p. 105.

7. Tom St. George, interview conducted by the author, January 1994. Mr. St. George has also worked as a dramaturg at several professional theaters.

8. Michael Feingold, interview conducted by the author, January 1994.

9. Ibid.

10. Gitta Honegger, interview conducted by the author, January 1994.

11. Ibid.

12. Lloyd Richards, interview conducted by the author, January 1994.

13. Feingold interview.

14. Honegger interview.

15. Ibid. The term "well-made play" is a translation of the French *piece bien faite*, and referred originally to a form of play, codified by Eugene Scribe (1791-1861), which thrives on causal events, logical resolution, and action which consistently meets audience expectations. The term has come into common theatrical usage referring to a play written according to the traditional formula.

16. Richards interview.

17. Ibid.

18. August Wilson, "The Ground on Which I Stand," p. 14.

19. Feingold interview.

20. Gerald Bordman, *The Oxford Companion to American Theatre* (New York: Oxford University Press, 1992) p. 718.

21. Don B. Wilmeth, *Cambridge Guide to American Theatre* (New York : University of Cambridge Press, 1994) p. 201.

22. Wilson, "The Ground on Which I Stand," p. 73.

23. Henry Louis Gates Jr., "Chitlin Circuit," p. 47.

24. Robert Brustein, "Subsidized Separatism," *The New Republic*, October 1996, p. 27.

25. August Wilson, interview conducted by the author, February 1994.

26. Wilson, "The Ground on Which I Stand," p. 73.

27. Wilson, "August Wilson Responds," p. 106.

28. Ricardo Khan quoted in Frank Bruni, "From the Wings, a Prayer: A Black Troupe Improvises," *The New York Times*, 12 February, 1997, Section C, p. 1.

29. August Wilson, interview conducted by the author, April 1997.

30. August Wilson quoted in Don Shirley, "Colorblind Casting Has Wilson Seeing Red," *The Los Angeles Times*, 1 September, 1996, Calendar Section, p. 46.

31. Wilson, "The Ground on Which I Stand," p. 16.

32. Wilson quoted in Gates, "Chitlin Circuit," p. 48.

33. Wilson, "August Wilson Responds," p. 106.

34. Wilson, "The Ground on Which I Stand," p. 71.

35. Micheal Scassera, "In the Driver's Seat, August Wilson and *Jitney*," *Performing Arts*, November 1997, p. 17.

36. Wilson interview.

37. Wilson, "The Ground on Which I Stand," p. 73.

Sources Cited

Bernstein, Richard. "Rescuing Black Voices from the Past." *The New York Times,* 27 March, 1988, Arts & Leisure Section, pp. 1 & 34.

Brown, Chip. "The Light in August," *Esquire,* April 1989, pp. 116-125.

Bruni, Frank. "From the Wings, A Prayer: A Black Troupe Improvises." *The New York Times,* 12 February, 1997. Section C, pp.1 & 16.

Brustein, Robert. "The Lesson of *The Piano Lesson,*" *The New Republic,* 21 May, 1990, pp. 28-30.

——. "Subsidized Separatism," *American Theatre,* October 1996, pp. 26-27 & 104.

Filichia, Peter. "*Jitney* Gives Audience a Joy Ride," *Newark Star Ledger,* 22 April, 1997, p. 17.

Freedman, Samuel. "Round Five for a Theatrical Heavyweight," *The New York Times,* 15 April, 1990, Arts & Leisure Section, p. 20.

Gates, Henry Louis, Jr., "Chitlin Circuit," *The New Yorker,* 3 February, 1997, pp. 43-50.

Gussow, Mel. "Fine Tuning the Piano Lesson," *The New York Times Magazine ,* 10 September, 1989, p. 18.

Hampton, Aubrey. "August Wilson: Playwright," *Organica,* Summer, 1988, pp. 24-27.

Jones, LeRoi. *Dutchman and The Slave.* New York: William Morrow and Co., 1964.

——. *Home: Social Essays.* New York: William Morrow and Co., 1966.

Marks, Peter. "Cabdriver's Melancholy Resists the Liquid Cure," *The New York Times*, 23 May, 1997, Section C, p. 3.

Neal, Larry. *Visions of a Liberated Future: Black Arts Movement Writings.* New York: Thunder's Mouth Press, 1989.

New Dramatists. *New Dramatists Fact Sheet.* New York: New Dramatists, 1994.

Program for the 1997 National Playwrights Conference. New York: Playbill, 1997.

Rothstein, Mervyn. "Round Five for a Theatrical Heavyweight," *The New York Times*, 15 April, 1990, Arts & Leisure Section, pp. 1 & 8.

Scassera, Michael. "In the Drivers Seat, August Wilson and *Jitney*," *Performing Arts*, November 1997, pp. 14-17.

Schwartzman, Myron. *Romare Bearden: His Life and Art.* New York: Harry Abrams, Inc., 1990.

Shannon, Sandra. *The Dramatic Vision of August Wilson.* Washington, D.C.: Howard University Press, 1995.

Shirley, Don. "Colorblind Casting Has Wilson Seeing Red," *The Los Angeles Times*, 1 September, 1996, Calendar Section, p. 46.

Tallmer, Jerry. "Hearing Voices," *Playbill* for *Two Trains Running*, April 1991, pp. 8-12.

Tomkins, Calvin. "Putting Something Over Something Else," *The New Yorker*, 28 November, 1977, pp. 53-61.

Watlington, Dennis. "Hurdling Fences," *Vanity Fair*, April 1989, pp. 102-10.

Weiss, Hedy. "A Playwright Pays Homage to a Painter," *Chicago Sun Times*, 22 September, 1991, Section E, p. 7.

Wilson, August. "August Wilson Responds," *American Theatre*, October, 1996, pp. 105-107.

———. *Fences*, version I. Unpublished property of August Wilson, 1982.

———. *Fences*, version II. Unpublished property of The Eugene O'Neill Theater Center, 1983.

———. *Fences*, version III. *Theater*, Summer/Fall, 1985, pp. 36-67.

———. *Fences*. New York: Plume Books, 1987.

———. "The Ground on Which I Stand," Wilson's keynote address of June 26, 1996, to the Theatre Communications Group National Conference, reprinted in *American Theatre*, September 1996, pp. 14-17 & 71-74.

———. *The Homecoming*. Unpublished property of August Wilson, nd.

———. "I Want a Black Director." In *May All Your Fences Have Gates: Essays on the Drama of August Wilson*. Nadell, Alan, ed. Iowa City: University of Iowa Press, 1994.

———. *Jitney*, version I. Unpublished property of August Wilson, 1979.

———. *Jitney*, version II. Unpublished property of August Wilson, 1996.

———. *Jitney*, version III. Unpublished property of August Wilson, 1997.

———. *Joe Turner's Come and Gone*, version II. Unpublished property of The Eugene O'Neill Theater Center, 1984.

———. *Joe Turner's Come and Gone*, version III. *Theater*, Summer/Fall, 1986, pp. 63-89.

———. *Joe Turner's Come and Gone.* New York: Plume Books, 1988.

———. *Ma Rainey's Black Bottom,* version I. Unpublished property of August Wilson, August 1981.

———. *Ma Rainey's Black Bottom,* version II. Unpublished property of the Eugene O'Neill Theater Center, July 1982.

———. *Ma Rainey's Black Bottom,* version III. Unpublished property of August Wilson, August 1982.

———. *Ma Rainey's Black Bottom,* version IV. Unpublished property of the Yale Repertory Theatre, 1984.

———. *Ma Rainey's Black Bottom.* New York: Plume Books, 1985.

———. *Mill Hand's Lunch Bucket (Joe Turner's Come and Gone,* version I). Unpublished property of August Wilson, 1983.

———. *Seven Guitars.* Unpublished property of August Wilson, 1995.

———. *The Piano Lesson.* New York: Penguin Books, 1990.

———. *Two Trains Running.* New York: Penguin Books, 1993.

INTERVIEWS CONDUCTED

Kirk Aanes, Playwright for whom August Wilson served as dramaturg at the Eugene O'Neill Theater Center's National Playwrights Conference; interview conducted January 1994.

Mary Alice, Actress who created the role of Rose in *Fences*; interview conducted January 1994.

Walter Dallas, Director for the premiere production of *Seven Guitars* and the Crossroads Theatre Production of *Jitney*; interview conducted April 1997.

Charles Dutton, Actor who created the roles of Levee in *Ma Rainey's Black Bottom*, Loomis in *Joe Turner's Come and Gone*, and Boy Willie in *The Piano Lesson*; interview conducted December 1993.

Michael Feingold, Dramaturg for the Eugene O'Neill Theater Center National Playwrights Conference's readings of *Ma Rainey's Black Bottom* and *The Piano Lesson*; interview conducted January 1994.

Gitta Honegger, Resident Dramaturg for the Yale Repertory Theatre for productions of *Ma Rainey's Black Bottom*, *Fences*, *Joe Turner's Come and Gone* and *The Piano Lesson*; interview conducted January 1994.

James Earl Jones, Actor who created the role of Troy in *Fences*; interview conducted December 1993.

Marion Isaac McClinton, Director of the Pittsburgh Public Theater's production of *Jitney*; interview conducted July 1997.

David Moore, Dramaturg for the Yale Repertory Theater's production of *Joe Turner's Come and Gone*; interview conducted November 1993.

William Partlan, Director for the Eugene O'Neill Theater Center's National Playwrights Conference's readings of *Ma Rainey's Black Bottom* and *Fences*; interview conducted November 1993.

Kim Powers, Dramaturg for the Yale Repertory Theatre's production of *Ma Rainey's Black Bottom*; interview conducted November 1993.

Lloyd Richards, Artistic Director of the Eugene O'Neill Theater Center, former Artistic Director of the Yale Repertory Theatre, and Director of the premiere productions of *Ma Rainey's Black Bottom, Fences, Joe Turner's Come and Gone, The Piano Lesson,* and *Two Trains Running*; interview conducted January 1994.

Amy Salz, Director for the Eugene O'Neill Theater Center National Playwrights Conference's reading of *Joe Turner's Come and Gone*; interview conducted November 1989.

Tom St. George, Playwright for whom August Wilson served as dramaturg at the Eugene O'Neill Theater Center's National Playwrights Conference; interview conducted January 1994.

August Wilson, interview conducted February 1994.

August Wilson, interview conducted April 1997.

172

Index

ABOUT THE AUTHOR

Joan Herrington has degrees from Wesleyan University (Connecticut), Hunter College, and UCLA, where she earned her doctorate in Theater History and Dramatic Literature in 1994. Previously on the faculty of the University of Redlands, she is now Assistant Professor of Theater at Western Michigan Universtiy.

Before beginning her teaching career, Dr. Herrington had practical experience in theater and film, having served as an off-Broadway drama critic, as Literary Manager at the American Place Theatre in New York City, and as an independent film producer on several feature films.

Her essays on August Wilson appeared in *May All Your Fences Have Gates: Essays on the Drama of August Wilson* (1993) and *August Wilson: A Casebook* (1994), and will run in forthcoming issues of *American Drama* and *Journal of Dramatic Theory and Criticism*. Her awards include a number of fellowships from UCLA in the early nineties and a Eugene O'Neill Theater Center Criticism Fellowship in 1982.

Dr. Herrington, her husband, and daughters Emily and Sarah live in Kalamazoo.